CULTURES OF THE WORLD
India

Marshall Cavendish
Benchmark
New York

PICTURE CREDITS

Cover: © PCL/Alamy
Anders Blomqvist/Lonely Planet Images: 17, 64, 105 • Andrew Bain/Lonely Planet Images: 122 • Andrew Parkinson/Lonely Planet Images: 45 • April Maciborka/Lonely Planet Images: 63 • Bedi/AFP/Getty Images: 48 Brent Winebrenner/Lonely Planet Images: 40, 62, 88 • Christer Fredriksson/Lonely Planet Images: 52, 67, 102, 120 • Christian Aslund/Lonely Planet Images: 54 • raig Pershouse/Lonely Planet Images: 59 • Dennis Walton/ Lonely Planet Images: 100, 126 • Dinodia Photos/Getty Images: 28 • Diptendu Dutta/AFP/Getty Images: 31 • Eddie Gerald/Lonely Planet Images: 60, 78 • Garry Weare/Lonely Planet Images: 6 • Gavin Gough/Lonely Planet Images: 30, 112 • Gerard Walker/Lonely Planet Images: 103 • Grant Dixon/Lonely Planet Images: 8 • Greg Elms/Lonely Planet Images: 82, 124, 125, 128 • Hira Punjabi/Lonely Planet Images: 46, 84 • Inmagine: 18, 23, 24, 26, 36, 37, 39, 47, 76, 85, 90, 92, 93, 94, 116, 119 • Izzet Keribar/Lonely Planet Images: 38 • John Sones/Lonely Planet Images: 14 • Johnny Haglund/Lonely Planet Images: 10, 12 • Keren Su/Lonely Planet Images: 50 • Marshall Cavendish International (Asia): 135 • Martin Hughes/Lonely Planet Images: 89 • Michael Steele/Getty Images: 113 • Nicholas Reuss/Lonely Planet Images: 44, 77 • North Wind Picture Archives: 25 • Patrick Horton/Lonely Planet Images: 96 • Paul Beinssen/Lonely Planet Images: 57, 98, 99, 114, 117, 127 • Paul Harding/Lonely Planet Images: 106, 109, 121 • Photolibrary: 1, 3, 5, 7, 9, 20, 42, 43, 55, 56, 58, 66, 68, 70, 71, 72, 108, 130, 131 • Raveendran-Pool/Getty Images: 33 • Raveendran/AFP/Getty Images: 34 • Richard I'Anson/ Lonely Planet Images: 16, 83, 101, 111 • Sara-Jane Cleland/Lonely Planet Images: 53 • Sipra Das/India Today Group/Getty Images: 32 • Tim Makins/Lonely Planet Images: 81 • Tom Cockrem/Lonely Planet Images: 69 • Tony Wheele/Lonely Planet Images: 13

PRECEDING PAGE

Children squeezed at the back of a rickshaw.

Publisher (U.S.): Michelle Bisson
Writers: Radhika Srinivasan, Leslie Jermyn, and Roseline NgCheong-Lum
Editors: Deborah Grahame-Smith, Stephanie Pee
Copyreader: Tara Tomczyk
Designers: Nancy Sabato, Bernard Go Kwang Meng
Cover picture researcher: Tracey Engel
Picture researcher: Joshua Ang

Marshall Cavendish Benchmark
99 White Plains Road
Tarrytown, NY 10591
Website: www.marshallcavendish.us

© Times Media Private Limited 1990. First Edition.
© Times Media Private Limited 2002. Second Edition.
© Marshall Cavendish International (Asia) Private Limited 2012. Third Edition.
® "Cultures of the World" is a registered trademark of Times Publishing Limited.

Originated and designed by Times Media Private Limited
An imprint of Marshall Cavendish International (Asia) Private Limited
A member of Times Publishing Limited

Marshall Cavendish is a trademark of Times Publishing Limited.

Library of Congress Cataloging-in-Publication Data
Srinivasan, Radhika, 1951-
India / Radhika Srinivasan, Leslie Jermyn, and Roseline Lum. — 3rd ed.
    p. cm. — (Cultures of the world)
 Summary: "Provides comprehensive information on the geography, history, wildlife, governmental structure, economy, cultural diversity, peoples, religion, and culture of India"—Provided by publisher.
Includes bibliographical references and index.
ISBN 978-1-60870-782-9 (print)
1. India—Juvenile literature. I. Jermyn, Leslie. II. NgCheong-Lum, Roseline, 1962- III. Title. IV. Series.

DS407.S74 2012
954--dc22   2011004346

Printed in Malaysia
7 6 5 4 3 2 1

CONTENTS

INDIA TODAY

INDIA IS REMARKABLE FOR ITS DIVERSITY, BOTH CULTURAL AND geographical. It is home to several ethnic groups, each with its own language and culture. The separate histories of these groups are, however, woven together in a tapestry that depicts the origins of some of the world's major religions—such as Buddhism and Hinduism—and the spread of others—such as Islam and Christianity. This variety of cultures and religions is reflected in the vibrancy and color of Indian music, dance, and festivals, and in the architectural styles of the country's majestic palaces and temples.

In geographical terms India is the seventh-largest country in the world. It boasts contrasting landscapes—high mountains and low river plains, deserts and tropical jungles—and a diversity of animals and plants that match the diversity of the people. With more than a billion people, India faces the challenges of providing everyone with an adequate living and of preserving nature's bounty.

Visitors to India are immediately assailed by the colors, sounds, and smells that epitomize India. Everything seems excessive: the crowds milling about, the noise of traffic and the human multitudes, and the disparity between the rich and the

Beautiful mountains of Himachal Pradesh.

poor. Outsiders are invariably overwhelmed by the shocking poverty that is immediately apparent on every Indian street. In 2010 it was estimated that more than 37 percent of Indians lived below the poverty line. More than 22 percent of the rural population lives in poverty, and this drives urban migration, contributing to the already densely populated cities. In spite of these difficulties, the Indian people go about their daily lives with serenity and a certain sense of resignation.

Despite its poverty, the Indian economy is the second-fastest growing economy in the world, after China's. The country's large population has translated into a large skilled workforce but unemployment still remains high. However, domestic demand has been increasing and the growing economy, along with a comparatively cheaper labor has attracted foreign investors.

India has a very diverse social, cultural, and political fabric and while it makes for a very rich culture and society, it also has resulted in violent and tragic clashes between different religious and ethnic groups. India's diversity is also reflected in its political landscape—the central government shares its power with the 28 states. India's political history has by no means been peaceful either.

Indians are justly proud of their ancient cultural heritage. They enjoy classical music and dance but at the same time embrace the modern comforts brought about by economic progress. In the cities the growing middle class finds pleasure in branded goods, fine wines, and imported automobiles. The influence of India can be seen through its cultural and culinary exports— Bollywood movies have been credited with the resurgence of musical film and theater in the Western world, and Indian cuisine can be found in practically every global city in the world.

However, cementing the social cohesion that is so typical of Indian society is the belief in traditional values of family and hard work. In its headlong rush toward progress, India retains its spiritual soul that is rooted in religious devotion and brotherhood.

Women collecting water from a well.

GEOGRAPHY

The Bhagirarthi River with the
Kalanag peak in the distance.

1

NDIA IS ABOUT ONE-THIRD THE SIZE OF the United States. With an area of 1.27 million square miles (3.3 million square kilometers), it is the seventh-largest country in the world. It is a subcontinent bounded by the Himalayas in the north and vast seas in the south. To the east is the Bay of Bengal, and to the west, the Arabian Sea. Both of these bodies of water stretch southward to join the Indian Ocean.

In India there is a great diversity of landforms such as lofty mountains, deep valleys, extensive plains, and a number of islands.

The Himalayan mountain range—one of the longest mountain chains in the world—extends over a distance of 1,490 miles (2,398 km) from the northern state of Jammu and Kashmir (which India and Pakistan both claim) to the eastern border state of Arunachal Pradesh. It should be noted that the Himalayan range includes the highest point on Earth—Mount Everest—that lies 29,029 feet (8,848 meters) above sea level.

At either end of the Himalayas are more mountain ranges. A few passes provide crossing points. In the course of its long and eventful history, the Indian

Right: A river winding through the valley in the Himalayan mountain range.

9

subcontinent lived under the threat of physical invasion, especially from armies using historical routes, such as the Khyber Pass (in the Hindukush Mountains) and Bolan Pass (in the Kirthar range in southern Pakistan).

Bhutan, Nepal, and China are India's northern neighbors; Afghanistan and Pakistan are situated in the northwest; Myanmar (Burma) and Bangladesh are located in the east. Sri Lanka lies to the south, barely an hour's boat ride from the subcontinent's southern tip. In the southeast, close to Indonesia, are India's Andaman and Nicobar islands.

A fisherman walking out to his nets on the Brahmaputra River.

MOUNTAINS AND RIVERS

India can be divided roughly into three geographical regions: the mountainous Himalayan north; the fertile Gangetic Plain, which is formed by the basins of three great rivers: the Indus, Ganga, and Brahmaputra; and the rocky Deccan south. The Indus flows mostly into Pakistan, whereas the Brahmaputra flows into Bangladesh, before reaching the Bay of Bengal. The Ganges, which Indians consider the holiest of rivers, flows from the Himalayas—through the states of Uttar Pradesh, Bihar, and West Bengal—and into the Ganges Delta, before draining into the Bay of Bengal.

Although the rivers in the north are snow-fed, most of the rivers in the south are rain-fed and fluctuate in volume. The Godavari, Krishna, Mahanadi, and Cauvery rivers enrich the soil in the southern region. The Gangetic Plain, fed by the Ganges River's abundant water supply, has rich alluvial soil and is one of the most fertile and densely populated tracts of land in the world. The triangular region south of the Gangetic Plain consists mainly of the rocky, uneven Deccan Plateau. Bordering this plateau on either side are smaller mountains, known as the Eastern and Western Ghats.

The Vindhya Mountains and the Narmada River stretch across the central area of the subcontinent, separating the north from the south. The presence of these two geographical features is a big reason why the histories of the north and south have often taken different courses.

This physical division probably also accounts for the different languages that Indians speak today. There are two language families in the country: the languages of the north—Hindi, Punjabi, Gujarati, and Rajasthani, for example—are generally descended from Sanskrit and are part of the Indo-European language family; the languages of the south—Tamil, Telugu, Kannada, and Malayalam, for example—are part of the Dravidian language family.

Although India has a long coastline (4,350 miles/7,000 km), it has few natural harbors. Changing sea levels in the past have shifted the country's coastline, and as a result, ancient ports, such as Tamluk in the east, Kaveripatnam in the south, and Lothal in the west, are landlocked today.

SEASONS AND CLIMATE

India's climate varies from torrid to arctic, depending on the region and the season. The country experiences six seasons during the year: summer, fall, winter, spring, summer, and winter. India's climate is affected by two seasonal winds—the northeast monsoon and the southeast monsoon. The northeast monsoon, commonly known as winter monsoon, blows from land to sea, whereas the southwest monsoon, known as summer monsoon, blows from sea to land after crossing the Indian Ocean, the Arabian Sea, and the Bay of Bengal. The southwest monsoon brings most of the rainfall during a year in the country.

The valleys of Kashmir and Shimla in the north of the country are delightfully cool in the summer months (April—June), but reach freezing temperatures in the winter months (December—January). New Delhi, also in the north, experiences thunderstorms preceded by dust storms in July and August.

In contrast the central and southern regions of India experience largely tropical weather. For Mumbai and the Western Ghats, the months of June to September are wet ones, when annual rainfall reaches 118 inches

(300 centimeters). Chennai and places farther south get more rain in December. In the hot season the weather can be oppressive, with temperatures rising as high as 122°F (50°C) in central India.

Rainfall also varies from region to region. In the eastern state of Assam, near the Khasi Hills, annual rainfall can be as high as 430 inches (1,092 cm). Cherrapunjee in the east holds world records for the most rain received both in a year and in a month—1,042 inches (2,646 cm) and 366 inches (930 cm), respectively.

Occasionally a shortage of rain leads to drought and famine, whereas excessive rain causes flash floods and the loss of lives. In an agricultural country such as India, the farmers are at the mercy of the weather. For this reason Indian farmers often pray to the rain god, Varuna, either to protect them from floods or to bless them with abundant rain.

NATURAL RESOURCES

India's varied climate supports a rich range of vegetation. The Himalayan region is wooded with pines and conifers, whereas eastern India has

A man caught in monsoon rains in Kolkata.

luxuriant forests and thick clumps of bamboo. The subcontinent boasts some 190 million acres (77 million hectares) of forests and 49,219 plant species, many of which are not found anywhere else in the world. There are several protected reserves, but trees are still being felled for fuel.

India is also blessed with a wide variety of mineral deposits, including iron ore, coal, lignite, silver, copper, gold, and zinc. Coal and peat provide for more than half of India's energy consumption; wood, oil, and natural gas provide for much of the rest, making the subcontinent almost self-sufficient in meeting its energy needs.

WILDLIFE

India is home to more than 500 mammal species and 1,228 bird species. Many of these animals, including wildcats such as the snow leopard and the spotted cheetah, are exclusive to the subcontinent. Some of them are endangered, and there are no fewer than 80 national parks, 440 sanctuaries, and 23 tiger reserves to protect these animals.

Elephants in the Periyar Sanctuary in Kerala.

India has one of the largest populations in the world—it has more than 1 billion people, second to China.

The Indian elephant is well known for its friendliness toward humans and for its role in temple and palace ceremonies. Wild elephants are so common in the Mudumalai sanctuary in the south and in the Assam forests in the east that they sometimes stray into houses and trample gardens! Elephant killing and the sale of ivory have been outlawed in almost every country in the world. Yet sadly many of these majestic creatures are still hunted for their tusks, which fetch a fabulous price on the black market.

The bison, buffalo, black buck, and nilgai (a type of antelope) are some other animals that are commonly seen in India. Rhinoceroses, jackals, and monkeys of different kinds are also found in the jungles of central India.

The birds that inhabit the subcontinent range from tiny sunbirds that are no bigger than butterflies to cranes and vultures. Wild peacocks, brilliantly colored pheasants, and fowl abound in the northern state of Rajasthan, where one can also see migratory Siberian cranes flying south to nest in December or January.

POPULATION

An official population census is carried out once every 10 years in India. In 2001 the population stood at 1,028,610,328. India is only the second country in the world, after China, to have grown to more than 1 billion people. A 2010 estimate put India's total population at 1,173,108,018.

Overpopulation is a major problem in a country where a third of the adults are illiterate, almost half the children are undernourished, and more than a third of the population lives in poverty. India is the second most populous country in the world, with a population growth rate of 27 million people per year.

India is still a predominantly rural country, with more than three-fourths of the population living in rural areas. Most of these people have minimal education and are engaged in farming. Only 28 percent of Indians live in urban areas.

The cities face urbanization problems. According to current estimates, Mumbai is the largest Indian city, with a population of more than 21 million. Each day thousands of people enter Mumbai in search of work. New Delhi, Kolkata, Chennai, and Bangalore are other overpopulated cities in India.

While cities such as Mumbai and Kolkata boast the luxurious mansions of movie stars and businesspeople, they also have thousands of very poor and ill-fed people living in shanty slums and on sidewalks.

INTERNET LINKS

www.ecoindia.com

This website introduces the national parks of India, with detailed information on their ecological systems, as well as other places of ecological interest. A comprehensive description of local plants and animals is also provided on this site.

www.mapsofindia.com

This website provides a brief overview of Indian geography, in addition to physical and political maps of India. It also features state maps, road networks, and railroads.

www.indiabook.com/india-information/indian-geography.html

This website furnishes a comprehensive introduction to Indian geography. Additionally some short accounts of other geographical facts, such as the physical features of India (mountains, rivers, and natural vegetation), climate, population, languages, and natural resources of the country have been provided at this site.

HISTORY

Statues carved into the facade of Cave 19 of the Ajanta Caves.

2

I NDIA'S PAST IS STRONGLY LINKED TO the Indus River, which flows about 2,900 miles (2,736 km) from Lake Mansarovar (in the Himalayas) to the Arabian Sea.

The Indians called the river Sindhu, whereas the Persians called it the Hindu and referred to India as Hindustan. However, it was the Greeks who pronounced *Sindhu* as Indus, from which the name India is derived.

India's history goes back more than 5,000 years. In the 1920s the ancient cities of Mohenjo-Daro and Harappa were discovered in what is Pakistan today. Two ancient sites in India are Ropar in Punjab and Kalilbangan in Rajasthan, along the Indus. Indications of an advanced civilization dating back to around 2500 B.C. have been found, such as brick houses, a well-planned drainage system, and script-bearing clay

The ruins of 15th-century Rana Kumbha Palace in Chittogarh, Rajasthan.

Ruins at the Mulgandha Kuti Temple where the Buddha was thought to have once meditated.

seals. Historians speculate that nomadic peoples settled along the river plain, perhaps imitating the success of earlier farming communities. The cycle of the Indus was crucial, because as the waters receded each summer, the rich alluvial soil that was left behind was eminently suitable for agriculture. How this farming lifestyle evolved into a sophisticated culture remains a mystery.

Historians in the 19th century theorized that the people of the Indus Valley were Dravidians and that Aryans (Indo-Europeans, possibly from Iran) came to the subcontinent around 1500 B.C. and mingled with the prevailing people. Due to a lack of direct evidence, however, many scholars today question this theory.

During the Vedic period, the four *Vedas* (vay-dahs)—Books of Knowledge—were written (*veda* is the Sanskrit word for "knowledge"). The Vedas contain hymns that address primarily the origin of life and the glorification of nature, personified as *devas* (day-vahs), or gods, such as Agni and Varuna, the gods of fire and rain, respectively. These gods were worshiped with rituals, sacrifices, and the recitation of the hymns, which priests today still chant during Hindu ceremonies in homes and temples.

BIRTH OF RELIGIONS

The ruling classes believed they were nobler than the laboring masses who cultivated the land. They divided society into four social classes, based on occupation: *Brahman* (brah-min), the priestly class; *Kshatriya* (shah-tree-yah), the ruling class; *Vaishya* (vy-shee-yah), the merchant class; and *Sudra* (sood-rah), the laboring class.

Gradually these class distinctions transformed into a broad system in which social, economic, and religious status became semi-hereditary and interacted in complex ways. The post-Vedic period saw the birth of many

THE BUDDHA

Prince Siddhartha Gautama was born in 624 B.C. in Lumbini, Nepal. He lived in luxury, married at age 16, and had a son. When Gautama was 29 years old, he discovered that there was much suffering in the world around him. Traditionally it is explained that he suddenly recognized the problems of sickness, old age, and death while visiting the city on his royal chariot. On the first day of his visit, he saw a very weak old man bowed over his walking stick. The next day he saw a sick man, lying on the road, and on the third day, he saw a dead body being taken for cremation. These three observations showed him that every stage in life is characterized by suffering. Because he believed in reincarnation, he realized that the only way to avoid the unending cycle of suffering was to remove oneself from the cycle of life, death, and rebirth.

Realizing the worthlessness of worldly pleasures, Prince Siddhartha's mind turned away from family, merrymaking, and politics. He was so moved by the suffering of people that he renounced everything and went in search of answers to his questions about the cause of human misery.

After a period of meditation, he received a vision of enlightenment and came to be known as the Buddha, "the one who knows."

Sanskrit works, such as the *Puranas* (poo-rah-nahs)—old world legends—and epic tales, such as the *Ramayana* (reh-MAH-yah-nah) and the *Mahabharata* (mah-hah-BHAH-reh-tah).

Rituals and animal sacrifices increased, in the belief that the gods could be appeased by them. Moreover two great religious thinkers were born: Vardhamana Mahavira, the founder of Jainism, and Siddhartha Gautama, the founder of Buddhism.

THE GREEK GIFT AND KING ASHOKA

In spring of 327 B.C., Alexander the Great, the Greek Macedonian invader, conquered the Persian Empire and marched into northwestern India as far

The Ashoka Pillar is the national emblem of India.

as the river Beas in Punjab. Although Alexander's victory was temporary and had little long-term political impact, the contact led to an exchange of ideas between India and the West for the first time.

In the northwestern regions Greek sculpture provided the model for Indian gods and goddesses. Almost 500 years after the Buddha's death, his images were created, first with Greek features and later in distinctly Indian styles. The Greek and Indian art forms became famous at two Buddhist centers, Gandhara and Mathura. Greek influence is therefore a landmark in the history of Indian art.

Politically, at this time, India was divided into many states, each ruled by a prince. The first king to unite the princely states and promote Buddhism both within and outside India was King Ashoka (reigned 272—232 B.C.), the third king of the Mauryan Dynasty.

Ashoka's violent war with the Kalinga kingdom (spanning Orissa and the region to its south) proved a turning point in his life. With thousands of casualties, the excessive bloodshed in the Kalinga War shocked his conscience and prompted him to adopt Buddhism. Almost overnight Ashoka became a Buddhist, spreading the message of peace and nonviolence. He inscribed Buddhist principles of morality on rocks and pillars and spent the remainder of his life performing acts of charity, helping the poor and the needy.

Buddhism spread to Sri Lanka, Central Asia, and Afghanistan, thanks to Ashoka's zeal. The Ashoka Pillar, now in the New Delhi Museum, is crowned with a four-headed lion and a chakra, or wheel, at the center. This is India's national emblem today, signifying spiritual fearlessness and diligence.

GOLDEN AGE OF THE GUPTAS

Almost immediately after King Ashoka's death in 232 B.C., the powerful Mauryan Empire began to disintegrate. Much of northern India became disunited and fell into the hands of foreign powers—the Persians, Huns, Scythians, and Sakas from Central Asia. Of these invaders, a nomadic tribe known as the Yueh-Chi advanced upon the northwestern frontiers and brought parts of China, Central Asia, Afghanistan, and northern India under a single rule. Kanishka, the Yueh-Chi king, is remembered chiefly for his role in taking Buddhism into the remote corners of Asia. He started the Saka era, which for a full thousand years was used as a standard for dates throughout Asia, just as the Christian era is used today as the standard for dates throughout much of the world.

After a gap of more than two centuries in political history, the strong Gupta Dynasty took over India and gave the country a long period of peace and prosperity. Chandragupta Vikramaditya (A.D. 380—413), the best-known Gupta king, was a great patron of art and literature. The poet and dramatist Kalidasa, the "Indian Shakespeare," born 12 centuries before the English bard, and the physician Charaka graced Vikramaditya's court. Kalidasa is considered the greatest figure in classical Sanskrit literature. Aryabhata, the mathematician who discovered the laws governing *shunya* (shoon-yah), or zero, and who explained the method of calculating eclipses, also came from this golden age of the Guptas.

SOUTHERN INDIA

Since ancient times southern India has enjoyed greater peace and stability than northern India. Tamil was and still is the language of the south. In fact it is the oldest living language in the world today.

Of the Tamil rulers the Pallavas and Cholas have left a lasting imprint on southern India. The Pallavas built the rock-cut shore temple at Mamallapuram near Madras (now Chennai) and reestablished the worship of Shiva and Vishnu. Shiva and Vishnu are the Hindu gods of destruction and preservation, respectively.

Many great Hindu temples and Buddhist monasteries were built during the golden age of the Guptas. Of these the 29 Ajanta caves in central India are the most outstanding. Carved out of solid rock, the walls and ceilings depict scenes from the Buddha's life. The paintings of the Ajanta caves provided the inspiration for the Dunhuang caves in China, the temple of Horyuji in Japan, and Buddhist cave paintings in Central Asia.

The Cholas are remembered for the magnificently constructed Hindu temples and bronze sculptures found in Tanjore, Kanchi, and Chidambaram. They also promoted music, dance, and learning throughout their united southern empire.

The Chola Empire extended as far south as Sri Lanka for a while, under King Rajendra Chola (reigned A.D. 1012—44). Chola also established trade links with China via Southeast Asia. Indian culture spread to most parts of Southeast Asia from the beginning of the fourth century A.D., but especially during Chola rule, between the eighth and eleventh centuries. Buddhist monasteries and Hindu temples in Java, Sumatra, Malaya, Thailand, and Cambodia revealed a strong Indian influence. Their language, literature, art, and political systems are also inspired by Indian models.

From the fourth to ninth centuries, southern India was the birthplace of many Tamil poet-saints (or devotional poets), who revived the people's faith in Hindu gods and goddesses. In addition to writing poems in praise of Vishnu and Shiva, these poet-saints (teachers and writers devoted to a divine principle) rejuvenated Hindu religious practices among Jain and Buddhist kings. The Alwars (Vaishnavaite saints) and Nayanmars (Saivaite saints) revitalized the Indian religious environment. They are still revered today in southern India.

MEDIEVAL INDIA

While southern India continued to enjoy considerable peace, northern India experienced several invasions after the ninth century. The kings of the northern Indian kingdoms remained divided and weak and could not resist Muslim attacks.

Arabs, Turks, Afghans, and Mongols made successive inroads into northern and western India. They plundered Hindu and Buddhist places of worship, removing vast treasures of gold and jewelry. Worst of all the looting was the sacking of the famous Somnatha temple in A.D. 1026 by the Afghan conqueror Mahmud Ghazni, who escaped with a huge amount of the temple's wealth of gold and jewels.

The only real resistance came from the proud Rajput warriors of western India. There are many tales relating the courage of Rajput women, who preferred to burn themselves alive rather than surrender to the Muslim invaders. However, even the fierce Rajputs could not withstand the Muslim attacks.

It was not until the 13th century that the Muslim invaders settled down and formed a stable government, the Delhi Sultanate. India was ruled by Turkish kings until 1398 when Timur (Tamerlane) led a Mongol attack and quickly destroyed Delhi. The sultanate survived but it took more than a century to rebuild the city. In 1525 it was Timur's descendant Babur who invaded India and brought Delhi into the Mughal Empire.

MUGHAL SPLENDOR

Babur's grandson Akbar the Great was the first Mughal king to extend his empire to cover the whole of northern and central India. He married a Rajput princess, showed great tolerance toward Hindus, and initiated a fusion of Hindu and Muslim art forms in architecture, painting, music, and dance.

A portrait of Mughal ruler Jalal Ud-Din Akbar.

Akbar (1556—1605) built the splendid city of Fatehpur Sikri near Agra. It had a hall called Ibadat Khana, in which people gathered to discuss various religious doctrines. Akbar blended the highest truths of Islam, Brahmanism, Christianity, Jainism, and Zoroastrianism, and formed a new religious faith named Din-i-Ilahi, or "religion of the world." It advocated 10 important virtues based on tolerance. His principles of tolerance formed fundamentals of the Indian constitution after independence. His son, Jahangir (reigned 1605—27), was fond of landscaping Mughal gardens into replicas of a Persian paradise.

Some of these gardens can still be seen in Udaipur and Kashmir. Jahangir also loved painting, and this led to the growth of many schools of miniature painting in India.

Jahangir's son, Shah Jahan (c. 1592—1666), is well remembered for the splendid forts and mosques he constructed at enormous cost. The most outstanding is the marble mausoleum called the Taj Mahal (Crown Palace), built by Shah Jahan as a memorial to his second wife, Mumtaz Mahal.

With the exception of Aurangzeb (1618—1707), Shah Jahan's son, the Mughal kings were great lovers of music. North Indian classical dance and music—once religious—became secular, having entered the Mughal courts. The North Indian style became distinctly romantic, with the introduction of elements of Urdu poetry.

However, the people became poorer, especially during the cruel reign of Aurangzeb. Heavy taxes and temple funds filled the royal treasury. Landless laborers and manual workers became bonded slaves, and crime increased in the rural regions. With his death, the mighty Mughal Empire started to collapse.

"If anywhere on Earth there is paradise, it is here, it is here, it is here."
—Jahangir, a Mughal emperor, on his visit to the Valley of Kashmir in the early 1600s

The mausoleum of Mughal emperor Akbar.

ARRIVAL OF THE EUROPEANS

In the early 17th century yet another foreign power entered India—the British. In 1600 Queen Elizabeth I granted a royal charter to a group of English traders to set up a trading company—the East India Company—in the East Indies (southeastern Asia including India, Southeast Asia, and the Malay Archipelago). The company's ships first arrived in India at the port of Surat in 1608. Sir Thomas Roe reached the court of the Mughal emperor Jahangir as the representative of King James I in 1615, and gained for the British the rights to establish a factory at Surat. This way the East India Company set up trading posts in Bombay (now Mumbai), Madras (Chennai), and Calcutta (Kolkata). The French, Dutch, and Portuguese (who had taken over Goa in 1510) established their own trading centers, buying textiles, tea, spices, gold, and silver cheaply in India and selling these goods at an enormous profit in Europe. The European trading stations grew into flourishing cities.

The British viceroy of India, Lord Curzon, entering Delhi with his wife on an elephant.

The British East India Company signed treaties with various Indian maharajas, or princes, who gave the British economic advantages and political power. The fall of the Mughal Empire, the divisiveness of the Indian kings, and the enterprising shrewdness of the British backed by military strength paved the way for a British Empire to develop in India in the 18th century.

BRITISH INDIA

Numerous small mutinies eventually culminated in the Sepoy Rebellion of 1857. The British had introduced Enfield rifles loaded with lubricated

Rebel sepoys (Indian soldiers serving in the British military) during the Sepoy Rebellion of 1857.

cartridges (made from pig and cow fat), the ends of which had to be bitten off before use—something both forbidden and insulting to Hindus and Muslims. To the Hindus, cows were sacred; to the Muslims, eating pork was forbidden. This was the final straw in a decade of discontent over the mistreatment of Indian soldiers by the British East India Company.

However, the rebellion was put down by July 8, 1858, and the British Crown took over the government of India, making India a British colony. The British introduced modern technology to manufacture goods, such as textiles and machines. They built railways to facilitate administration; established factories, schools, and universities; and introduced the Western concept of democracy. They also encouraged evangelistic missionary activities and the spread of Christianity by reaching out mainly to the low-caste Hindus.

MODERN INDIA

At the start of the 20th century some liberal British policies brought social and economic reforms. The British initiated constitutional changes and

EARLY REFORM MOVEMENTS

The 19th century saw the growth of many political, social, and religious reform movements. Raja Ram Mohan Roy started the Brahmo Samaj in 1828 to fight social ills such as the caste system, child marriage, superstitions, and suttee, or the practice in which Hindu widows would burn themselves on their husbands' funeral pyres. Ramakrishna Paramahansa (1836—86), a Hindu mystic, preached that the true worship of God lies in the service of humanity. His disciple, Swami Vivekananda (1863—1902), established a Hindu order called the Ramakrishna Mission in May 1897 and awakened the conscience of Indians.

local self-government at the village level and recognized the newly formed political party, the Indian National Congress. English education created Indian intellectuals who craved India's freedom.

At this time Mohandas Karamchand Gandhi (1869—1948) was becoming a household name in India. Gandhi was born to a Hindu family in Porbandar in the Indian state of Gujarat. Gandhi—better known by his title of *Mahatma*, meaning "great soul"—spent around 20 years in South Africa, then returned to India to fight for India's independence. He advocated *satyagraha* (seht-yah-grah-hah), nonviolent resistance for justice to gain independence for India from the British Empire.

Gandhi advocated peaceful strikes. He persuaded his followers to wear Indian handloom textiles instead of English cloth. He walked hundreds of miles in silent protest against the British tax on salt, forcing the removal of the tax. Gandhi's nonviolent strategy made British attempts to subjugate the resistance through military power almost impossible.

The British—who ruled over India for nearly 200 years—finally gave in, and India gained independence on August 15, 1947. Jawaharlal Nehru (1889—1964) became India's first prime minister. However, because Hindu and Muslim leaders could not overcome their differences, India was partitioned, and Pakistan was born. The partition resulted in the world's largest mass

Mahatma Gandhi is still one of the most respected figures in India today.

movement of people accompanied by unprecedented genocidal violence, as Hindus and Muslims murdered each other. Gandhi's assassination by a fellow Hindu in 1948 contributed to the turmoil that engulfed the country.

INDIA POST-INDEPENDENCE

Since independence the Indian political landscape has been dominated by the Gandhi-Nehru family and the Congress Party. After Nehru's death in 1964, Lal Bahadur Shastri took over. In 1966 Nehru's daughter Indira Gandhi (1917–84) was elected prime minister, and she ruled the country on and off between 1966 and 1984. On Wednesday, October 31, 1984, when Indira Gandhi was going to her office, she was gunned down by her own bodyguards. Her son Rajiv Gandhi (1944–91) succeeded her, but he too was assassinated by a member of the Liberation Tigers of Tamil Eelam (LTTE), a terrorist group. After losing the elections in 1996, the Congress Party came back to power in 2009 with another Gandhi at the helm, Rajiv's widow, Sonia Gandhi. Although they do not hold any government posts, Sonia and her son Raul wield enormous political influence in the country.

According to a 2010 report, apart from the leftists, all political parties in India are dominated by powerful families, with as many as 1,000 families having secured their succession lines. Even at the village level, sons and daughters of the powerful often "inherit" seats that are vacated by their parents.

Although India has witnessed enormous economic progress since the 1990s, the country is still plagued by social problems such as the great divide between the rich and the poor and ethnic tensions between Hindus and Muslims. Terrorist attacks since 2005, both homegrown and foreign-sponsored, not only take a heavy toll on the population but also fuel tensions with neighbors, especially Pakistan.

INTERNET LINKS

www.indhistory.com

This website provides a detailed account of Indian history, which is divided into three parts: ancient, medieval, and modern. In addition this site features a page on gods and goddesses as well as background information about Indian culture and festivals.

www.indohistory.com

This is a comprehensive website on the various periods of Indian history, with timelines of the Indian subcontinent. This site also includes a description of the formation of the Indian states as well as the political administration of the country.

www.mkgandhi.org

This site is maintained by the Gandhian Institute, and features writings and photos as well as audio recordings of the great advocate for nonviolence. The aim of this nonprofit organization is to disseminate Gandhi's views on nonviolence and to encourage students to work for peace in the world.

GOVERNMENT

The Secretariat Parliament Building in New Delhi.

3

INDIA BECAME A SOCIALIST DEMOCRATIC republic on January 26, 1950. The country has a parliamentary system of government. Its 28 states and 7 union territories are governed by the central cabinet according to the constitution adopted in 1950. Each state has its own government, but the union territories are administered by the president through an appointed administrator.

The structure of the Indian government is similar to the British system. Its parliament comprises two houses—one is directly elected by the people and the other by appointment.

The president, elected for a period of five years by members of parliament and state legislative assemblies, is the head of state and the constitutional head of the executive, legislative, and judicial branches of government. The president is also the commander of the armed forces—a ceremonial post—and acts on the advice of the central cabinet.

The central cabinet is headed by the prime minister. The real powers lie with this executive body. The central cabinet is responsible

Right: An election official explaining the procedure of casting electronic votes to residents in Milanmore village before state assembly elections in West Bengal.

Members of Parliament Sahnawaz Hussain (*left*), Sharad Yadav (*center*), and C.P. Thakur (*right*) on their way to a parliamentary session.

to the House of the People, or the *Lok Sabha*, which consists of 545 seats. Elections to the Lok Sabha are held every five years.

Legislative powers are the domain of the parliament—consisting of the Lok Sabha and the nominated members of the *Rajya Sabha* (Council of States, having maximum strength of 250 seats)—that acts as a forum of public opinion. The judicial branch protects the constitutional and statutory rights of Indians.

The executive, legislative, and judicial branches work together to prevent the misuse of power. For example the judicial arm aims to guard against the executive branch assuming powers beyond those outlined in the Indian constitution.

THE FEDERAL SYSTEM OF GOVERNMENT

The constitution of India provides for a federal system of government similar to that of the United States, with the federal government at the center

"The State shall not deny to any person equality before the law or the equal protection of the laws within the territory of India." —Equality as entrenched in the Indian constitution

and a similar structure in the states. This decentralizes power and permits easy administration.

Each state has its own governor as the constitutional head, the chief minister and their council to work as the state executive, and the elected members of the legislative assembly. While the federal government covers important areas such as defense, foreign affairs, and communications, the state is given autonomy in several areas, including agriculture, internal law and order, and public health. This power structure continues all the way down to the districts and villages.

In a similar manner the hierarchy of the Supreme Court, High Courts, subordinate courts, and the district or village courts helps dispense justice at various levels. To ensure uniformity the constitution has allowed for a single system of courts to administer both national and state laws.

Since people of different religions live in India, the constitution has set different personal laws to help solve problems relating to family matters, such

Prime minister of India, Manmohan Singh (*right*), with prime minister of Pakistan, Yousuf Raza Gilani (*left*), at the start of the 2011 International Cricket Council World Cup.

"India is a geographical and an economic entity, a cultural unity amid diversity, a bundle of contradictions held together by strong but invisible threads."
—Jawaharlal Nehru, India's first prime minister

as marriage, divorce, and succession. The Hindu Marriage Act of 1955, for instance, cannot be applied to Muslims, whose laws of marriage follow the Hanafi doctrines of Sunni law. Similarly different acts apply to Christians and Parsis.

United Progressive Alliance chairperson Sonia Gandhi (*center, in red*), with her son and Congress Party secretary general Rahul Gandhi (*center, left*).

THE CONSTITUTION

Many of India's policies have been guided by its constitutional principles. The constitution of India—based in part on the constitution of the United States—guarantees equality before the law and equal protection under the law, and prohibits discrimination on the basis of religion, race, caste, sex, or place of birth. It also guarantees basic rights such as freedom of speech, assembly, association, religion, movement, and residence, and upholds the right to acquire property and to practice a profession or trade. In 1976 the constitution was amended to include the fundamental duties of each citizen. These fundamental duties ensure that every citizen abides by the constitution, defends the country in times of crisis, and promotes harmony among all regions and religions. Since its inception there have been 94 amendments to the constitution.

LOCAL GOVERNMENT

In rural India the basic unit of government is the *panchayat* (pehn-chah-yeht) or village council. Literally meaning an "assembly of five persons," panchayats can be made up of any number of members, all popularly elected for five years. Councillors elect a council chair among themselves, and this person represents the village in the block council. A block is a grouping of 200 to 600 villages. At the top of the three-tiered system of local government sits the district council, which brings together all block council chairs from the district. There are 636 districts (according to a 2010 estimate) in India, distributed among the states and union territories. The role of the *panchayat* is to uplift the lives of rural Indians in areas such as sanitation, education, and family welfare.

The urban agglomerations are divided into municipalities whose members are also directly elected for a period of five years. Town councillors elect one of their members as mayor or council president. However, all executive power is in the hands of the municipal commissioner, who is appointed by the state governor. The municipal government is responsible for education, health, sanitation, safety, and maintaining roads and other public facilities. Municipalities have been financially independent and self-sufficient since 2000.

INTERNET LINKS

www.india.gov.in

This is the national portal of the Indian government, which reproduces the constitution of the country and details the roles of the Indian government. This site also includes basic information on all the states and union territories.

www.indian-elections.com

This website provides comprehensive write-ups on the electoral systems in India as well as all the political parties jostling for power in the country. Also featured are the results of the most recent state and national elections.

www.parliamentofindia.nic.in

This site is devoted to both houses of parliament and the presidency, in addition to detailing the roles of each house and the differences among them. The section on the president includes photos, speeches, as well as an interesting write-up on the presidential palace.

ECONOMY

Farmworkers picking green pea pods to sell.

4

INDIA HAS A MIXED ECONOMY. STATE-owned industries and enterprises include transportation, communications, armaments, mining, electricity, power, as well as commercial and district banks. The private sector handles consumer products, textiles, IT services, and electronics, among others.

Successive five-year plans have helped the Indian economy grow steadily since the inception of the first Five-Year Plan in 1951. The objective of the current 11th Five-Year Plan (2007—12) is to increase GDP growth to 10 percent as well as to create 70 million new jobs. In addition the plan aims to reduce the infant mortality rate and malnutrition among children and to raise the standards of primary education.

Economic liberalization, including privatization of state-owned firms and relaxed rules on foreign investment, has brought about much progress, turning the country into the world's 12th-largest

Right: Farmworkers threshing wheat to separate the chaff from the wheat grains.

economy. Since the beginning of the 21st century GDP growth has averaged 7 percent. The star performer of the Indian economy is the services sector. Employing only one-third of the workforce, it accounts for more than half of total output.

INFRASTRUCTURE, MONEY, AND TRADE

A wide network of railways and roads links all of India's regions, while a vast number of cargo carriers passes through the country's ports. The national carrier is Air India, and it plies both domestic and international routes. In addition a number of private low-cost airlines, each based in a different city, offer domestic flights.

India's currency unit is the rupee. Approximately 45.39 rupees equaled US$1 in December 2010. The Reserve Bank of India operates as the central bank, issuing notes and controlling the mint. As of December 2009, India's foreign exchange and gold reserves amounted to more than US$274 billion.

Public transportation in India is so packed that commuters even climb on top of buses!

Exports dropped by about $40 billion from 2008 to 2009, accompanied by an even sharper drop in imports. India exports mainly agricultural produce, textiles, chemicals, leather goods, iron, steel, and precious stones. It imports mainly crude oil and petroleum products, machinery, fertilizers, and chemicals. The IT industry—software design and manufacture and call centers—is a large earner of foreign exchange. Projected earnings for the sector in 2012 are in excess of $100 billion.

ENERGY

Most of India's electricity is produced using coal and petroleum products. About 25 percent is generated by hydroelectric power, and 4.2 percent is generated by India's 19 nuclear power plants located mainly in the north and west of the country. Nuclear energy is slated to play a bigger role in satisfying the demands for electricity, with more plants in the pipeline. In 25 years' time, nuclear energy will account for 9 percent of total electricity production.

Pandoh Dam near Tandi in India. Hydroelectric power constitutes about a quarter of India's energy.

India produces methane from animal waste, industrial discharge, and domestic sewage. These waste by-products are recycled even further into enriched fertilizer. The All India Coordinated Biogas Program was started in 1975, and today millions of biogas plants have been installed all over the Indian countryside.

In line with its conservation policy, India is tapping into the sun's energy to provide solar lighting for houses and solar-powered drinking water systems. With about 300 clear and sunny days a year in most parts of the country, solar power holds enormous potential for India. Under the Solar Mission Plan issued in 2009, India aims for 20-gigawatt power capacity by 2022.

About 70 percent of India's energy needs are met through indigenous production. However, India still imports petroleum products for its growing energy needs, mainly from oil-producing countries of the Middle East, including Iran, Iraq, and Saudi Arabia. Even then the supply of electricity to households still falls short by as much as 12 percent during peak consumption hours.

AGRICULTURE

India is primarily an agricultural country, with 60 percent of the population engaged in farming. The agricultural sector contributes 20 percent of the total gross domestic product and accounts for 10 percent of export earnings. India is not only self-sufficient in rice and wheat, but also exports its excess production of food grain.

Although farmers in some parts of India still use the antiquated bullock (or bull)-drawn plow, many have made the transition to modern farming methods, using tractors, mechanized watering equipment, and pesticides and fertilizers. This has greatly increased grain production over the years.

However, India continues to import sugar, oils, and other commodities, as its own production is insufficient to meet domestic demand.

A welder at work.

INDUSTRY

India is one of the top 10 industrial economies in the world, with the manufacturing sector posting a 16 percent growth in the first quarter of 2010. Computers, IT hardware and software, petroleum products, leather goods, and garments head the list of industrial exports.

Other important Indian industries are tea-processing, sugar, silks and woolens, vegetable oils, paper, pharmaceuticals, and the manufacture of electronic goods. Many consumer items are manufactured locally, including electrical goods, motor vehicles, television sets, video recorders, and computers.

India ranks among the leading producers of iron ore, coal, and bauxite, and is a significant producer of copper, mica, asbestos, chromium, gold, as well as silver.

INTERNET LINKS

www.ibef.org

This website provides detailed and up-to-date information on various sectors of the Indian economy. The site also details economic features and growth potential for each state and includes a section on sustainable development.

www.agriculturalproductsindia.com

This is a comprehensive website on agricultural production in India, including its history and the importance of water management in farming. The site also gives a list of all the agricultural products of India.

www.indiaenergyportal.org

This site details the various types of energy sources in India, with statistics on power production by type. It also includes links to various websites with information on energy for children.

ENVIRONMENT

Pangong Tso Lake in Ladakh,
Jammu and Kashmir.

5

INDIA IS HOME TO MANY PLANTS AND animals. It is not easy to balance the needs of the huge human population against the needs of nature. The Indian people and their government have made a strong commitment to preserving the subcontinent's natural treasures.

INDIA'S NATURAL DIVERSITY

India's varied landscapes form distinct ecological zones with unique flora and fauna. Tropical rain forests flourish in the northeastern parts of the subcontinent; thorn forests grow in Gujarat and Rajasthan; and tropical deciduous and dry alpine forests cover the Himalayan foothills. Mangrove forests line the coasts. Living in these habitats are 500 mammal species, 408 types of reptiles, 1,228 bird species, 197 amphibian species, 57,000 species of insects, 2,546 varieties of fish, and about 15,000 flowering plants.

Right: **The Valley of Flowers in Uttaranchal in Northern India.**

Today, however, some 300 animal species in India are considered endangered. Despite the country's history of environmentalism and its cultural heritage of respect for living things, human development trends have created conflicts between the people and the wildlife. The government passed the Environment Protection Act in 1986 (last amended in 1991) with the objective of providing for the protection and improvement of the environment. Moreover numerous laws have also been enacted to reduce pollution and conserve the natural biodiversity.

ENDANGERED MAMMALS

ASIATIC LION Asiatic lions look similar to their larger African cousins, except for their slightly shaggier mane and larger tail tuft. Asiatic lions once lived in an area that stretched across Southwest Asia from northern Greece to central India, but extensive hunting in the last century has severely depleted their numbers worldwide. Today their only natural habitat is the Gir Forest Sanctuary in the Indian state of Gujarat. From a low of 177 in 1968, their population has grown steadily to 411 in 2010. India banned lion hunting in the 1950s.

A majestic Asiatic lion. Asiatic lions can only roam freely in the Gir Forest Sanctuary.

Yet even in their home in the Gir Forest Sanctuary, the world's last Asiatic lions live an uneasy existence. They share their home with native herdsmen and their cattle. These herdsmen destroy the forest by felling trees for fuel and timber. They also kill lions to protect their cattle—the lions' alternative food source when natural prey, such as deer, is hard to find. Lions generally avoid contact with people, but they occasionally attack people when they are provoked or injured.

There are laws protecting the Asiatic lion, but plans to set up a second reserve have encountered stiff resistance from the people of Gujarat. Helping the lion population regenerate is a mammoth task. The Delhi Zoo's lion-breeding program, initiated in 1959, welcomed its first lion cub only in 2000.

BENGAL TIGER   Before 1900 India had between 80,000 and 100,000 tigers. Hunted for their skin and other body parts, these tigers dwindled in number to around 40,000 before 1947 and to 1,800 by 1971. India launched a tiger habitat conservation program entitled Project Tiger in 1973 with the help of the World Wildlife Fund (WWF) that has proved to be one of the rare successes in the fight against extinction. Today there are 27 tiger reserves in India. The number of tigers in the wild has rebounded to 3,500, but the species is still on the endangered list because the animal is still being poached relentlessly for its bones and skin.

SLOTH BEAR   This nocturnal bear weighs 175 to 310 pounds (79—141 kilograms). It has a coat of black and brown fur with white fur across the chest and on the face. Its mobile snout is ideal for sucking up termites, its main food. The sloth bear inhabits the forested areas south of the Himalayas. It is also found in Sri Lanka, Bhutan, and Bangladesh. It is protected by Indian and international laws, but the main threat to its survival is the destruction of forests caused by logging and agriculture. Poaching is another threat, with adults being killed for their body parts and cubs being captured and trained to perform in bear dancing shows. The current sloth bear population in the Indian subcontinent is estimated to be a little over 4,000, and the bears' population is rapidly declining.

PYGMY HOG   This is the smallest species of pig in the world, weighing only 10 pounds (4.5 kg). It was once thought to be extinct in India but was

A 19-month-old Bengal tiger. Despite numerous tiger reserves and conservation efforts, the Bengal tiger is still endangered—it is poached for its bones and skin.

The sloth bear population is threatened by the destruction of its habitat via deforestation and poaching.

rediscovered in northwest Assam in 1971. The pig lost a lot of its grasslands habitat to cattle grazing and human harvesting of thatch for houses. Listed as critically endangered, the species is on the brink of extinction, with only 250 adult hogs living in the area around Manas National Park in northwestern Assam.

GANGES RIVER DOLPHIN   This freshwater dolphin lives in the Ganges, Brahmaputra, Karnaphuli, and Meghana rivers. Water pollution, habitat fragmentation by dam projects and barrages, and direct killing of dolphins for their meat and oil have reduced India's once flourishing dolphin population to less than 2,000. Because the dolphins migrate seasonally, it is difficult to set up sanctuaries for them. Further study is thus needed to come up with a way to protect this unique animal.

ENVIRONMENTAL THREATS

SETTLEMENT   The natural environment suffers wherever there is human activity. As populations grow and people have to look for new places to set

"It shall be the duty of every citizen of India ... to protect and improve the natural environment including forests, lakes, rivers and wildlife, and to have compassion for living creatures."
—Article 51A of the Indian constitution

Trees being cleared to make way for a road in Arunachal Pradesh.

up homes, virgin forests are cleared to make way for buildings and roads, and land and marine resources are gradually drained to provide food and other materials for the human settlers.

The Indian people are largely rural and depend on farming for survival. As they look for land to plant food crops and rear animals, they take more and more space away from animals, the land's original inhabitants. Some wild animal species have stopped breeding because of human interference. Others, such as the Asiatic wild ass and the Gaur (Indian bison), contract diseases from domesticated horses and cattle. Still others, such as the tiger and the Asiatic lion, are killed when they prey on livestock.

POACHING Many animals are hunted for their skins and body parts. Poachers have killed the Indian rhinoceros for its horn, the Asian elephant for its tusks, and the tiger and snow leopard for their pelts. Some of the body parts of the Asiatic black bear and the sloth bear are prized as food delicacies and medicines.

THE WORST INDUSTRIAL ACCIDENT IN HISTORY

Bhopal is a city in Madhya Pradesh whose name has become synonymous with tragedy and the dangers of the use of toxic chemicals.

On the evening of December 3, 1984, at the Union Carbide Corporation's dry-cell battery manufacturing plant in Bhopal, water leaked into a storage tank containing methyl isocyanate gas (MIC), a very toxic chemical. Reacting with the water, the chemical vaporized and was carried on the wind to neighboring communities. The chemical's effects were immediate. Residents who did not die in bed staggered into the streets, blinded and choked by the gas. Many were rushed to the nearest hospitals, only to die after having suffered extended pain from inhaling the gas.

Following the accident Union Carbide closed the Bhopal plant. Five years of legal action resulted in the corporation agreeing to pay compensation to the Indian people for the loss and suffering caused by the accident. In 1989 the Supreme Court of India ordered Union Carbide to pay US$470 million in settlement of claims arising from the tragedy. Union Carbide later sold its interest in the Bhopal plant and contributed the proceeds to a charitable trust set up to fund the building and operation of a hospital for the victims.

Unfortunately little could be done to alleviate the environmental consequences of the 1984 accident. Toxic waste left at the Union Carbide factory has leached into the ground and polluted the wells from which the local people get drinking water. In 1999 Greenpeace, an environmental organization, reported excessive levels of a suspected carcinogen in water samples collected from the site (although tests by the Indian National Environmental Engineering Research Institute found no contamination in 100 off-site wells).

Bhopal has undoubtedly paid the world's highest price for a lesson on the environmental danger of toxic chemicals. The Madhya Pradesh state government reported that the accident resulted in approximately 3,800 deaths. Some 2,720 people suffered total or partial permanent disability, and 18,922 suffered permanent injury. The extent and severity of the Bhopal tragedy earned it a record for being the worst industrial accident in history.

Unfortunately poached items can be sold at extremely high prices to collectors of animal trophies and to consumers of medicines made from animal body parts. This makes the illegal trade in endangered animals very lucrative.

AGRICULTURE To divert water to agricultural areas, some 4,525 dams have been built, 73 percent of which are in the states of Maharashtra, Madhya Pradesh, and Gujarat. Dams destroy the environment by flooding river valleys, causing silt to build up downstream and animals to move out of the area or die due to changes in marine ecology.

In a bid to increase food production, India joined the Green Revolution. The introduction of high-yielding varieties of seeds and the increased use of fertilizers and irrigation are collectively known as the Green Revolution, which improved agriculture and helped India to become self-sufficient. Farmers were given special seeds that grew faster and produced more grain than the local varieties of food crops. However, these super seeds needed

Farmworkers transplating rice seedlings into the rice fields.

chemical fertilizers, pesticides, and herbicides to grow well. These chemicals washed into the rivers, polluting the water and harming marine wildlife. The speedy growth of the special seeds also reduced soil fertility. The rice fields were flooded all year-round to keep up with the increased pace of production. Thus the land had no time to lie fallow and rejuvenate after each harvest.

ENVIRONMENTAL PROTECTION

CHIPKO—THE "TREE-HUGGERS" OF NORTHERN INDIA In 1973 government attempts to fell trees in the Himalayan forests to get railroad ties and pulp wood for paper production were squashed by the Chipko Movement. The local people, many of whom were women and children, literally hugged the trees to stop the loggers' axes. This is how the movement got its name (*chipko* means "embrace"). This is also probably where the use of the term *tree-hugger* to refer to an environmentalist originated. The Chipko Movement spread throughout the Himalayan forests, making it impossible for the government to carry out its logging plans. Finally, in 1980, Prime Minister Indira Gandhi issued an order prohibiting logging in the region for 15 years. This was a major victory for the demonstrators. The ideals and practices of the movement have since spread to the forested regions of central and south India and to the states of Himachal Pradesh, Karnataka, Rajasthan, and Bihar. In March 2004 the surviving members celebrated the 30th anniversary of the movement with a procession from the village of Laata to Reni, where the original Chipko action took place. The government authorities were criticized, however, for hijacking the celebrations.

INTERNET LINKS

www.iucnredlist.org

The IUCN Red List of Threatened Species™ provides taxonomic information, conservation status, and distribution information on plants and animals. The list is maintained by the International Union for Conservation of Nature. Animals are categorized from "vulnerable" to "critically endangered," with in-depth analysis of the major threats to specific species.

www.indianwildlifeportal.com

This website lists all the national parks and wildlife sanctuaries in India, highlighting the major attractions. Also included in the site are write-ups on the important animals of Indian fauna.

www.indiawaterportal.org

The India Water Portal (IWP) routinely conducts user surveys either as focus groups, online surveys, telephonic conversations, or face-to-face interviews. This site covers every aspect of water in India, from wastewater management to drinking water. Also included in the site is a write-up on climate change as well as reports and articles on dams and floods.

INDIANS

An Indian woman from Madhya Pradesh in traditional dress.

6

INDIA IS ONE OF THE WORLD'S MOST ethnically diverse countries. Attempts have been made to bring ethnic groups together and create a national identity, but tensions between groups often end in violence.

It is almost impossible to categorize Indians by their racial origins. It is currently accepted by historians that an early Aryan civilization—dominated by peoples whose language connected them to the people of Iran and Europe—came to occupy northwestern and what was then north-central India roughly between 2000 and 1500 B.C. They then moved southwest and east, imperiling the indigenous groups of those areas. Many years of invasions by other cultures followed, adding to the ethnic diversity of India.

Thus present-day India includes a number of ethnic groups. Broadly speaking the people in the north and northwestern regions of Kashmir, Rajasthan, Punjab, and Delhi tend to resemble European and Indo-European peoples. They are usually tall and fair, with pronounced features. The central regions of Uttar Pradesh, Madhya

Right: Rajasthanis in their brightly colored clothing.

Pradesh, and Bihar are inhabited by people who are generally somewhat darker and shorter.

A blend of Dravidians, or indigenous Indian peoples, and Mongolians live in the eastern Indian regions of Assam, Manipur, Nagaland, and Mizoram. A Tibeto-Burman type characterized by slanting eyes and high cheekbones can be found in the Himalayan foothills.

PEOPLE OF THE KASHMIR VALLEY

The Kashmiris and Himachalis of the north, blessed with a healthy, cold climate, are energetic, robust, and exuberant. Muslims, Hindus, and Buddhists live harmoniously in these Himalayan valleys.

Jammu is the land of warriors called Dogras and shepherd-nomads called Gujars. Both men and women of Kashmir wear *phiran* (fee-rahn)—a long woolen cloak—and *salwar* (sehl-WAHR), or loose pants. The women wear headdresses and large silver earrings. Muslim men wear a cap and sport a

"A nation's culture resides in the hearts and in the soul of its people."
—Gandhi

Kashmiri workers taking a break and listening to a cricket game on a portable radio.

beard, whereas Muslim women often wear a black veil, the burka, which covers them completely.

In winter Kashmiris keep warm with a kind of portable heater. They place a *kangri* (KAHNG-gree)—an earthen pot of burning coals—in a cane basket. They tie this around their waist and then cover themselves with a cloak or shawl that traps the heat.

Kashmiris have long-established traditions of carpet and silk weaving, lacquerware, and wooden handicrafts. They cultivate apples, corn, and legumes in terraced fields cut out of hills, and grow flowers and vegetables on floating rafts called *radhi* (rah-di). Some live in houseboats known as *shikaras* (shee-KAH-rahs).

A group of children at the Golden Temple in Punjab.

Culturally the Himachalis have much in common with the Kashmiris. In the northern plateau of Ladakh, however, live some mountain-bound groups, mostly Tibetan Buddhists, whose isolation has helped them maintain their unique customs.

PUNJABIS AND RAJASTHANIS

Punjab, known as the land of the five rivers and traditionally India's breadbasket, is the most fertile state. Punjabis are primarily agriculturalists who grow wheat, rice, legumes, and vegetables. Punjab is also known for its hosiery, woolens, and excellence at sports.

Punjabis are tall and fair-skinned. The men wear loose white pants or the traditional lungi also called *tehmat* (teh-meht), made of extravagant silks in an endless variety of hues and shades—called dhoti throughout India, and *veshti* (vehsh-ti), *mundu* (moon-do), or *soon* (soon) in the south—with a

Rajasthani men usually sport mustaches and brightly colored turbans.

long shirt and a colorful turban. The women wear heavily embroidered long skirts or the Punjabi suit—loose pants and a long blouse—and usually cover their heads with a scarf or a shawl. Both men and women in the countryside love to adorn themselves with jewelry.

South of Punjab is Rajasthan, land of forts, palaces, deserts, and camels. Rajasthanis are famous for brassware, marble work, pottery, jewelry, embroidery, and painting.

Rajasthani women wear *ghagra* (GHAH-grah) or *lehenga choli*—gathered skirts that sweep the ground—and *kanchli* (kehnch-lee) or embroidered blouses. They cover their heads with brightly printed veils called *odhni* (odenee) and wear heavy jewelry. Rajasthani men wear loose dhoti or *churidar* (chew-ree-dahr)—tight pants—and a vest with a distinctive cut. They usually sport impressively huge mustaches and colorful turbans. Warm and good-natured, the people of Rajasthan take pride in their simplicity, honesty, and thrifty habits, the latter being almost proverbial among all Indians.

PEOPLE OF INDIA'S HEARTLAND

The largely Hindi-speaking northern and central states of Uttar Pradesh, Madhya Pradesh, and Bihar are the most densely populated regions of India. The heartland's rich mineral deposits have given rise to iron and steel industries, oil refineries, chemical plants, fertilizer factories, and paper industries, which in turn employ large numbers of people.

A group of young dancers from Madya Pradesh.

The rural people of India's heartland are primarily agriculturists who grow, among other crops, sugarcane, wheat, rice, and lentils. The farmers of central India rely heavily on the fertile soil of the Gangetic Plain for their livelihood. The rain-fed rivers Son, Ken, and Betwa supplement the Ganges and Yamuna rivers in watering the central farmland.

The people of the Bastar hills and the Chattisgarh plains in the central state of Madhya Pradesh hunt and work in the forests. The people of Chota Nagpur in the state of Bihar are farmers who still adhere to the archaic methods of cultivation that their ancestors practiced.

The inhabitants of India's heartland wear light clothing—generally cotton—because of the heat. Men in the rural areas wear the ubiquitous dhoti with a shirt, whereas the women wear traditional Indian clothing and decorate themselves with elaborate jewelry (as do women all over India). Jewelry is not just for decoration; it is also a form of savings that can be pawned or sold in an emergency. Only widows abstain from any form of ornamentation.

Both men and women in the cities favor Western-style attire—shirts and trousers, blouses, and pants or skirts. Young children generally wear as little as possible to stay comfortable in the heat, especially when they play.

India's heartland is also known as the pious heartland. Several religious centers such as Varanasi, Badrinath, Prayag, and Mathura—to which Indians frequently go on pilgrimage—are located in this region.

EASTERN INDIANS

The eastern states of Assam, Meghalaya, Nagaland, Manipur, Tripura, and Arunachal Pradesh are inhabited by several groups, including the Khasis, Garos, Jaintias, Mundas, Nagas, Ahoms, Bodos, Wanchos, and Miris. Each group has its own language, customs, and dress. The women of Mizoram and Nagaland wear a tight sarong wound around them like a dress. In Assam the women wear a *mekhela* (meh-khay-lah), or long skirt, and a *retir* (reh-tir), or blouse.

Dense hilly jungle and marshland thrive in the eastern states, where mineral deposits are abundant. Rice is the chief crop; the Assamese also

Kimchungru tribesmen celebrating the Hornbill festival in Nagaland.

grow tea. Bamboo work, cane products, and weaving are important cottage industries, and every home has a loom so the women can supplement the family income. The women of the eastern groups play a larger role than the men in both the fields and the home.

Culturally eastern Indians have much in common with their Burmese and Nepalese neighbors.

PEOPLE OF BENGAL, SIKKIM, AND ORISSA

Kolkata, the capital city of West Bengal—vibrant with lovers of literature, music, and the arts—has its unfortunate side. It is an example of the gaping disparity between the very rich and the very poor. Kolkata's poor are homeless pavement dwellers who lead a miserable existence on the roads and under the bridges of the city. Poverty has driven many of them to steal and beg. Yet Kolkata is also the place where some of India's wealthiest Bengalis reside.

A grandmother with her grandchild in Sri Kola, West Bengal.

Many Bengalis in the countryside are engaged in farming and fishing. They live in huts with sloping thatch roofs. Men wear a dhoti and a *kurta* (kur-ta), or long shirt, whereas women wear a sari, usually white with a colored border. Bengalis love to decorate the floor at the entrance to their homes with traditional designs called *alpana* (ehl-peh-nah).

North of West Bengal is the tiny Himalayan state of Sikkim, inhabited by Lepchas, Bhutias, and Nepalese. They wear handwoven clothes, drink yak's milk, and grow fruits, potatoes, cardamom, and barley.

Orissa, south of West Bengal, is famous for sculptured temples, dance, painting, and silver filigree. Well-endowed with rivers, it is a fertile coastal plain with large groves of coconut, mango, and palm, and fields of rice and sugarcane. Mining and jute-growing are other important occupations.

SOUTHERN INDIANS

Southern Indians are the Tamils of Tamil Nadu, the Telugus of Andhra Pradesh, the Malayalees of Kerala, the Kannadigas of Karnataka, and the Tulus of the Malabar Coast.

In the countryside Southern Indian men wear a small dhoti that resembles a loincloth. They are often bare-chested and barefoot. The women wear a sari with a short blouse. Elderly women, with earlobes stretched by heavy earrings, often wear no blouse, covering themselves

A traditionally dressed Goan woman.

deftly with just the sari.

The farmers of the region grow mainly rice, sugarcane, and coconuts. Some villages specialize in weaving, pottery, metal casting, or stone sculpting.

People in the southern cities reflect a mixed taste for modern and traditional values and customs, including dress; one may see women in a sari, hair decked with flowers, going to work in a modern office. Classical music or dance lessons for every girl is the norm, while great importance is attached to education, especially in Kerala, the city with the highest literacy rate in India.

WESTERN INDIANS

Western Indians are the people of Gujarat, Goa, and Maharashtra; Parsis who originally came from Persia; Portuguese of mixed descent; or Caucasians who settled in western Indian ports.

Gujarati villagers grow rice, wheat, corn, sugarcane, cotton, groundnuts, and sunflower seeds. The women wear a heavily embroidered *ghagra* and a short blouse, and their heads are generally covered with a veil cloth called *odhni* or *dupatta*. Gujarati men, especially from Kutch, wear tight white pants, gathered near the ankles. Their unique colorful vest is now a pan-Indian fashion.

Maharashtra's hilly Western Ghats are very fertile, being fed by a number of rivers. Rice, groundnuts, tobacco, and the famous Alphonso mangoes are grown here, in addition to cotton, the main crop. Rural Maharashtrian women tie their saris trouser-style, and wear large nose rings that dangle to the chin. The Goans and the women of Daman and Diu islands wear a knee-length sari as well as a Western-style skirt and blouse. Many men have discarded traditional clothes for shirts and trousers.

Mumbai, the capital city of Maharashtra, known as the Gateway of India, is the country's most important industrial city, besides being its biggest port and the nerve center of India's business and finance. Being influenced by the name Hollywood and being the major hub of Indian Hindi film industry, Mumbai is often informally cited as Bollywood. Residents of the city are cosmopolitan, and many adopt a Western lifestyle and outlook. The city has distinct Maharashtrian, Gujarati, Parsi, Tamil, and Sindhi areas.

INTERNET LINKS

www.ecoindia.com/tribes

This website details nine of the major tribal groups in India, explaining their geographical distribution, religions, and customs and festivals.

www.joshuaproject.net/countries.php?rog3=IN

This page from the Christian initiative Joshua Project gives a list of all ethnic minorities in India, detailing their numbers, geographical locations, languages, and religions.

www.webindia123.com/india/people/costumes.htm

This website provides a comprehensive description on Indian traditional attire. It also includes a description of traditional costumes presented in a lucid manner.

LIFESTYLE

The crowded streets of Varansi.

7

Though officially abolished, the caste system still has an invisible presence in Indian society.

CHANGE COMES LAST AND LEAST TO the countryside in traditional societies such as India. Rural life is a regular pattern of sowing, reaping, praying, and celebrating at family and social gatherings. These simple, repetitive acts have acquired a symbolic meaning over the many centuries of India's history.

The family plays a vital role. An Indian family is usually a home of three generations, rooted in a particular community. The family is also where traditional arts, handicrafts, and trades are learned and passed down. The cohesiveness of the family fosters a strong sense of belonging, and belonging is a serious and exacting concern in India. The family belongs to a particular lineage or *gotra* (go-trah) and is identified with a particular clan or *jati* (jah-ti) within a specific caste of a region or *kul* (kool). Through marriage, usually planned by collective choice over individual preference, families strengthen their bonds of lineage.

Family connections are seldom lost, even when a person leaves the village for the city in pursuit of a higher education or better job prospects.

Right: Families form the cornerstone of Indian society.

ARRANGED MARRIAGES

The concept of arranged marriages may sound impractical to the Western world, but in India, it is the norm. No matter how Westernized India may have become, arranged marriages are still viewed as the preferred choice in Indian families. Arranged marriages protect family links, which are very important to people in India. Parents look for suitable life partners for their children from families of the same religion or caste. Because young Indians seldom marry outside their own religion or caste, couples can avoid problems that are usually caused by social or economic disparities. Through an arranged marriage, two families enter into a mutual relationship. When problems do arise in the marriage, both families try to work together to help the couple.

THE PATRIARCHAL SYSTEM

Indian society is generally patriarchal. It is usually the man who exerts ultimate authority in the family's formal relations. The father, more than the mother, has control over the children. In some instances he makes the

"Some like to define India by its contradictions and extremes. It's a land of tolerance, but also a place where bitter rivalries . . . occasionally explode."
—Christopher Kremmer, Australian writer

It is usually the father who exercises supreme authority in the household.

important family decisions for as long as he lives, even after his son has reached adulthood.

The wife and mother, however, retains dominion over informal decisions both inside and outside the home. Together she and her husband maintain the stability of the family.

Before 1955, when the Hindu Marriage Act prohibited polygamy—marriage to more than one woman at the same time—a man could have more than one wife. In many remote villages polygamy still exists and goes unnoticed. Polygamy is legal only among Muslims, because their religion allows it.

When it comes to having children, boys are preferred, since many Hindu rituals require a male to fulfill obligations to the ancestors. Double standards still exist for boys and girls within and outside the home. For example parents would much rather spend money on higher education for their sons than for their daughters. In addition men are favored by professional employers.

Things are changing slowly, at least in the cities, because of industrialization, equal education opportunities for women, and exposure to Western ideas. These trends are giving urban women greater power in the family and, gradually, in the economy.

THE CASTE SYSTEM

The caste system was a social institution that divided Indian society into distinct groups. Its legacy is still apparent in many regions. In addition to the four main castes, there are hundreds of subcastes.

Although the caste system gave order to life and prescribed a code of conduct for everyone, many felt that it tended to emphasize social disparities and render the underprivileged vulnerable to exploitation. The Brahmans had access to knowledge and could thus advance to become society's elite. The Vaishya and Sudra were divided into some 3,000 subcastes, which were actually industrial guilds. The lowest social order included the garbage collectors, sweepers, and butchers—the "outcastes," or untouchables. Mahatma Gandhi called them *Harijan* (hah-ri-jahn)—children of God.

Today special attention is given to the needs of the economically backward groups, but caste consciousness is difficult to erase. In some villages Harijan are barred from drawing water at public wells or entering the inner sanctum of temples. Caste may be a consideration when it comes to marriage, especially in the south. Brahmans may choose to marry within their caste, as may the Chettiar moneylenders of the south and the royalty of Rajasthan. Caste identification still persists in several parts of India regardless of any personal qualities and achievements that an individual may have. A person's neighborhood, lifestyle, food habits, speech patterns, style of dress, and family name all indicate his or her caste and lineage. However, caste discrimination is waning. For example intercaste marriages based on mutual love are on the rise, especially in the cities.

THE CHANGING FACES OF WOMEN

Household responsibilities are largely the woman's domain in Indian society, as is still the case in many other cultures. In arranged marriages the bride's family usually has to pay the groom's family a dowry—a gift of gold, clothes, consumer durables, or large sums of cash—that can leave a poor family debt-ridden.

A Brahman priest performing a ritual. Even though the caste system has been officially abolished, it still persists in some of Indian society.

However, the situation is improving vastly for women in India. For example suttee—the medieval and scattered practice of widows burning themselves on their husbands' funeral pyres—has almost disappeared, and more widows are remarrying. Purdah—a system that discouraged men from addressing upper-class women without a veil or screen between them—is almost nonexistent today.

Women in some Dravidian societies, especially in Kerala and Manipur, enjoy considerable freedom and equality. In Kerala it is common for the man

With more girls attending school and joining the workforce, the role and position of women in society is changing considerably.

to marry into the woman's family, and property can pass from mother to daughter. The women of the Meitei tribe in the Imphal Valley of Manipur also command greater socioeconomic power than women elsewhere in India. Some of them have settled in the states of Assam and Tripura. There are even priestesses in the Manipuri tradition.

In the fast-changing cities of India, the role of the working woman is a contradiction. Economic independence and the popular women's liberation movement have given Indian women a new sense of freedom and confidence. However, heavy demands on them at work and at home have also given rise to conflicts, increasing the rate of divorce. A number of women's periodicals discuss modern issues, from fashion to premarital sex to drugs. At the central and state levels, too, women are making a difference. Women vote and hold important political positions. The gender gap in India is narrowing bit by bit. Moreover a considerable number of urban women are university graduates, and many of them choose careers in medicine, academia, and law. Women in India have gained empowerment and are moving at par with men in male-dominant Indian society.

CHILDHOOD

The moment of an Indian child's birth is marked on an astrological calendar, and the child's horoscope is charted. A boy will inherit family skills and honor the household gods. A girl teaches family traditions to her children. The birth of a son is generally considered a more celebrated event, because it brings the family a potential income earner.

A mother and her baby in Tamil Nadu. Naming ceremonies are an important part of a child's life, though the ritual varies from community to community.

Indian naming ceremonies vary from region to region. Generally on the 11th day after birth—a few days later in some communities—the child is dressed in fine clothes and blessed with a name. The name is written on a mound of paddy (unhusked rice) or wheat, and the baby is placed on it for a while. Only then is the child believed to have overcome afterbirth complications. For Indians human birth and plant life are analogous, and a successful birth is likened to a successful harvest.

Every milestone from then on is an occasion to celebrate, a rite to be performed, whether it is weaning from breast milk, taking the first step, ear piercing, head shaving, or the first birthday. Astrologically auspicious dates and times are selected for such events. The first step toward formal education is significant. The Hindus call this *vidyarambha* (vid-yah-rehm-bhah); the Muslims call it *bismillah* (bis-mill-lah). The Muslim priest helps a child recite a Koranic text and solemnizes formal learning.

In orthodox Hindu groups a boy's initiation is as vital as the start of his student life. The thread ceremony, called *upanayanam* (oo-pah-neh-yehm), among the warrior, priest, and merchant castes, symbolizes spiritual rebirth. Amid Vedic chants the boy undergoes rites to cleanse his body and mind. He is given three sacred threads to wear across his left shoulder for the rest of his life.

A Hindu girl does not go through such formal initiation. However, in many Dravidian societies, the first time a girl menstruates is celebrated with feasting and anticipation of her marriage.

TRADITIONAL MARRIAGE

Orthodox Hindus believe that an unmarried person has no social status. A Hindu marriage is considered a lifelong partnership, a sacred and unalterable union. Rarely is a traditional marriage entrusted to the whims of the boy or girl. The parents arrange the alliance after consulting the family elders and astrologers; matching horoscopes; and comparing castes, status, and family backgrounds.

The marriage ceremony itself is rich in symbolism, and preparations usually begin weeks before the event. Ritual practice may vary in detail from region to region, but the Vedic ritual itself has remained unchanged for more than 2,000 years.

A couple at their wedding ceremony at the Meenakshi Temple. The Hindu wedding ceremony is complex and has deep significance.

A priest conducting marriage rites.

Constructing a temporary altar to the fire god Agni, the priest acts as Brahma, the creator. The bride and groom are also likened to Indian gods and goddesses: Shiva and Shakti or Vishnu and Lakshmi. The marriage is complete when the groom ties a sacred thread, called *mangalasutra* (mehng-geh-lah soo-trah), around the bride's neck, after which the couple walks around the fire and recites the marriage verse from the Rig Veda. Blessings are then bestowed upon them by all the elders present in the ceremony.

The union is thus sanctified, making divorce unthinkable in the Indian tradition. There is no equivalent for the word *divorce* in the dictionary of any of the Indian languages. *Talaq* (tah-lahk), meaning "divorce," is used freely in Hindi, but it is an Arabic term imported by Muslims, for whom divorce is allowed, although strongly discouraged.

MODERN MARRIAGE

In the cities long years of formal education have pushed the marrying age into the late 20s and the 30s. When following the traditional path of finding a partner, young urban Indians may find the classified advertisements in the newspapers' special matrimonial columns an efficient matchmaker.

The practice of paying a dowry in marriage is losing its relevance in modern life and is a legally punishable offense. Mainstream India has completely weaned off dowry marriages in favor of love marriages.

Some modern families do not mind intercaste, interregional, or even interreligious marriages, when the man and the woman have known one another for years, either at college or at the workplace. Indira Gandhi, a Hindu, married a Parsi. Some people prefer to remain single, and a handful experiment with living together without a formal commitment.

"Take seven steps with me, my friend. Be my mate and blend with me."
—A marriage chant

Educated Indians today have modernized the external forms of marriage. An urban Indian couple retains the basic Vedic ritual, but holds the wedding reception at a five-star hotel.

OLD AGE

Old age is a beautiful stage of life in traditional India. When a son marries and adds to the family community, his parents move up the ladder of seniority and are consulted on all important family matters. In due course even neighbors and friends will seek their blessings on auspicious occasions.

The elderly are respected and their blessings and opinions are often sought by younger family members.

In ancient times, when a man and his wife grew old, they were expected to give up the materialistic family life and settle in a forest, practicing a simple, spiritual way of life. Today, although the elderly do not go to the forest, they do make pilgrimages to religious centers and gradually relegate mundane household affairs to the younger generation. Seldom is there a clash of interests between the old and the young; where resentment exists, it is rarely revealed, out of respect for the elders.

In the cities younger family members often prefer to set up their own homes, either to be closer to their workplace or because the joint family structure no longer appeals to them. Families meet only during festivals and family celebrations. Retirees feel less inclined to rely on their children, and a growing number save up for their future. However, although they are more self-reliant financially, the aged in the cities are less prepared emotionally. They face very real problems of loneliness, due to the breakdown of the extended family.

THE HINDU VIEW OF LIFE AND DEATH

Because reincarnation is a basic tenet of Hinduism, to the Hindu, life is an endless cycle of events that begins where it ends. Death is merely a stage in

A body being cremated along the Ganges River.

that cycle, as inevitable as birth itself. Therefore death is not final; it is just a transfer of the soul from one body to another, quite like taking off old clothes to wear new ones.

Whether one is reborn as a plant, insect, animal, or human being, and whether one's new life is a happy and prosperous one or filled with trials and tribulations depends on one's previous life. Hindus believe that a truly noble life, with good thoughts, words, and deeds, will release the soul from the life and death cycles and secure eternal liberation, called *moksha* (mohk-shah). The Buddhists call this nirvana—attaining a state of nothingness.

While Hindus perform several rites during their lifetime, surviving relatives perform last rites for a person's well-being in the next life. Failure to perform these rites would cause their soul to wander without a place in the next world. Only a son can perform the last rites for his father, which explains some of the traditional bias for sons.

The eldest son usually performs the last rites with the help of a priest. The dead body is dressed in new clothes, placed on a bier, and taken to the cremation grounds, amid the chanting of God's name. The pyre is lit, the body cremated, and the ashes collected the next day for immersion in the holy Ganges River. Thirteen days of mourning follow, to be completed with a ritual and a feast, both of which suggest a return to normality.

Although cremation is the norm among Hindus, young children and persons who are held in very great reverence are buried; so are Muslims and Christians. Victims of epidemics are generally cast away in water so as not to offend the evil spirits that have attacked the victim.

KARMA

Karma is a fundamental belief among Indians, especially Hindus and Buddhists, that means "action." Like the principle of cause and effect, good turns fetch a reward of good life, whereas bad words and deeds affect not just this life but the next as well. Logically, therefore, a person's birth in this life is determined by the cumulative good or bad actions of his or her previous lives.

Karma offers explanations for the inequalities of life—such as why one person may be born poor or handicapped or may suffer a series of hardships, whereas another, even if born to the same family, enjoys peace and prosperity. Karma blames humans themselves, not God, for their state of poverty or ignorance.

Belief in karma has generally made Indians passively accept their state of poverty. Although belief in karma does not mean a fatalistic pessimism, many people ascribe the events in their lives to it. Karma allows them to face those hardships they cannot avert without flinching.

Indians also believe that stars and planets affect the individual, and that the elements of earth, water, fire, wind, and space rule a human being's health and well-being. Many of their beliefs have foundation in the ancient sciences of astrology and medicine. In Indian society, where faith involves belief in the supernatural and myths are still alive, faith often gets mixed with strange superstitions.

SUPERSTITIONS

Indians may use the Gregorian calendar for their daily transactions, but when it comes to buying property, starting a business venture, or even moving house, they go by the Indian astrological calendar. In this even numbers are regarded as auspicious. Generally eight and nine are good, whereas seven is not. Wednesday is good for traveling and Friday is good for sacred matters. On Friday meat is taboo, a visit to the barber frowned upon, and visiting the home of a bereaved person is simply out of the question.

Sometimes these customs and beliefs degenerate into downright superstition. For instance if someone sneezes before a project starts, it will not be completed; if a lizard falls on one's head, death is imminent; if a dog howls, it is the call of Yama, the god of death. The list is endless. No one knows how some of these superstitions came about, but the Puranas tell frightening tales of what befalls those who do not believe in ancient practices.

These old stories also prescribe antidotes. Thus practices such as bathing in the holy Ganges River to wash away one's sins, or offering one's hair to God as a symbol of sacrifice, may appear superstitious to some but are religious obligations for the millions of people living in India.

In some isolated communities strict taboos are observed when events happen out of the ordinary, such as untimely deaths or epidemics. Belief in the occult is still strong, and witch doctors perform regular rituals and sacrifices.

VILLAGE LIFE

Except for a few regional differences, village life is basically the same all over India. Villagers wake up at dawn and take a quick bath before breaking their fast. On special days villagers, especially in the south, massage oil over their bodies and rinse with indigenous herbs and powders. The laundry is done by beating the clothes on rough stones and scrubbing them with soap.

For breakfast coffee is the beverage of choice in the south, whereas tea is standard in the north. Seated on the floor, Indians eat either food leftover from the previous night's meal or porridge made from rice, millet, or wheat. Then the men proceed to the fields or workplace, the children to schools, and the women set about the housework.

Everyone returns before sunset to tend to the cows and goats in their sheds, play traditional games, watch television, or attend temple festivals. There is plenty of leisure time for entertainment and social interaction. Evenings are for gossiping about politics or village affairs. Then, after checking that the animals have been fed and the water pots filled for the next day's chores, the villagers go to sleep on mats spread out on the floor.

CITY LIFE

City life in India presents many sharp contrasts. Apart from the wealth and poverty revealed by the coexistence and juxtaposition of slums and luxurious mansions, the city centers are generally congested.

High demand and short supply have created shortages of housing, water, electricity, telephone service, transportation facilities, and places in schools and universities. With better education more Indians now seek employment abroad, especially in the United States, Malaysia, and Singapore. More money to spend has led to growing consumerism.

Yet life in Indian cities can be rewarding. The people are caring and warm. Whether they are reaching out to a neighbor or extending hospitality to a stranger, Indians respond readily, almost instinctively.

Urban dwellers are increasingly becoming lovers of classical Indian art, making the cities vibrant with music and dance festivals that last several weeks in some seasons. The growth of art institutions reflects a growing interest in art among Indian youths. It has even become fashionable to use ethnic textiles and folk handicrafts. India's age-old traditions look set to live on into the information age.

INTERNET LINKS

www.indianchild.com/indian_villages.htm

This website describes the dynamics of typical villages in India and how the caste system pervades village life. This site also contains pages on children and family life.

www.aprendizdetodo.com/wedding

Set out like a film script, the description of a Hindu wedding ceremony on this website details the costumes of the participants, their responses, and behavior.

www.indianetzone.com/women

This site looks at the role of Indian women in ancient times as well as today, and their importance in the freedom struggle. The site also highlights a number of women who have been instrumental in the fight for gender equality.

RELIGION

The Golden Temple in
Amritsar in Punjab.

8

NDIA IS A SECULAR COUNTRY. THE assimilation of various religious values has generally created tolerance among the different groups. However, religious unrest does occur and has been a problem when politicians have exploited the people's religious differences.

Most clashes occur between Hindus and Muslims, the largest religious minorities in India. The destruction of the 16th-century Babri mosque in Ayodhya on December 6, 1992, by a political rally led to one of the deadliest riots in many major Indian cities.

The world's major religions have found a home in India, where Hinduism and Buddhism were born. Nearly 80 percent of the population is Hindu, with the rest professing to be followers of Islam, Christianity, Sikhism, Buddhism, Jainism, Judaism, or Zoroastrianism.

Religion plays an important part in Indian life. Joyous occasions are celebrated with a visit to a mosque, temple, or shrine, and it is common for Indians to make religious processions and pilgrimages, regardless of what faith they profess. Virtually every day of the year marks a festive occasion on the calendar of one faith or another.

Right: **The statue of Ganesha at the Parawrameswar Temple being washed.**

The intricate detail of the Kapaleeshwarar Temple in Chennai.

Indians display symbols of their faith at the front door of their home to invoke blessings from the gods and heavenly protection over the household. Christians adorn their doors with the cross, Muslims with a verse from the Koran, and Hindus with a picture of Ganesha, the god who wards off evil.

HINDUISM

Hinduism is one of the oldest living faiths in the world and forms the ethos of the majority of Indians. Unlike many other faiths, Hinduism does not have a founder. Nor is it based on any single scripture. Indians call it *Sanatana Dharma*—the faith with no beginning and no end.

Hinduism offers different approaches to persons of different aptitudes. It does not prescribe rules. Rather it reveals profound truths about life and suggests various paths of righteous living. As the choice of a path is left to the believer, the religion means different things to different people. One can understand aspects of the religion by examining its essential features, starting with the Vedas. These are sacred texts containing hymns of creation, prayers, and philosophical discussions.

To simplify high philosophy and offer it to the common people, legends were created. The Puranas, the Ramayana, and the Mahabharata are religious scriptures, containing spiritual and philosophical concepts that drive home universal values of righteous living.

A part of the Mahabharata is the Bhagavad Gita, a philosophical song of God that brings out the essence of Hinduism in simple form. Here Lord Krishna advocates three paths: the path of mental discipline for the intellectual (*jnana yoga*), the pursuit of love and devotion for the emotional (*bhakti yoga*), and the path of selfless service (*karma yoga*) for those who believe that "work is worship." In addition, for all people, Lord Krishna advocates nonviolence, truth, and detachment.

"India has 2 million gods, and worships them all. In religion all other countries are paupers; India is the only millionaire."
—Mark Twain, American author and humorist

HINDU VALUES   Hinduism does not deny one the enjoyment of life. It advocates the pursuit of four goals: *dharma* (dhahr-mah), *artha* (ahr-thah), karma, and *moksha*. These translate roughly as righteous living, wealth and prosperity, love and happiness, and release from the cycle of births and deaths.

Hindus strive to pursue the right action at the right time. Life is roughly divided into four stages: childhood, a time of joy and innocence; student life, a time of discipline in mind and body; married life, a time for family and the household; and old age, a time to renounce material things in preparation for the final years. Since these stages are common to everyone, Hindu priests can also marry and raise families.

Hindu gods and goddesses reflect the Hindu value system. Anything beautiful, valuable, or awe-inspiring is associated with divinity. Plant and animal life, natural forces of energy, the sun, the planets, the elements, art, knowledge, wealth, and happiness all have their corresponding deities.

Amid this host of gods and goddesses is the concept of the Hindu Trinity: Brahma the Creator, Vishnu the Preserver, and Shiva the Destroyer. Together they symbolize the ultimate god known as Brahman, represented by the formless sound symbol, *om* (ohm). (Brahman should not be confused with the priestly caste known as Brahman.)

Although Hindus believe that all these gods are different manifestations of one supreme God, the deities are very real to them. The gods' birthdays and marriage anniversaries are occasions for celebration in homes and temples. Hinduism really comes alive during such festivals.

HINDU RITUALS AND BELIEFS   Rituals are part of the Hindu way of life. From birth to death Hindus must observe various ceremonies in order to achieve total development. Although some of these rituals and customs are now obsolete, many are followed to this day. These rituals are imbued with rich symbolism. Each is a prayer for prosperity and offspring in this life and the next.

The cow is sacred to Hindus. They worship it as the Divine Mother, so eating beef is taboo. (This taboo was one of the sparks of the Sepoy Rebellion of 1857.)

During the popular Ganapati festival in Maharashtra and Durga Puja in West Bengal, huge images of deities are installed and consecrated. This is known as the life-giving ceremony. After 10 days of prayers and offerings, the images are taken on a procession and ceremonially immersed in a river, pond, or sea, suggesting a renewal and rebirth for the gods.

The cow is the source of life-sustaining milk and the symbol of fertility. Every animal, in fact, is associated with a god: the elephant with Ganesha, the snake with Vishnu, the bull with Shiva, the peacock with Murugan, the swan with Brahma, and so on. This association of gods with animals is one of the reasons why many Hindus are vegetarians. Some Hindus refrain from meat by choice, others because of caste considerations.

Water is sacred to Hindus. Many pious Hindus feel blessed after a dip in the river, in particular the Ganges. Most temples have a pond in the courtyard for bathing.

BUDDHISM

Buddhism was founded in the sixth century B.C. and spread across the whole of Asia. However, it was eclipsed as a distinct religion in India some time around the 12th century A.D. Many Buddhist ways were absorbed into Hinduism, and the Buddha became one of the incarnations of the Hindu god, Vishnu.

The 1950s saw a Buddhist revival movement led by Dr. B. R. Ambedkar, as a result of which there are more than 8 million Buddhists in India today. Most of them live in the state of Maharashtra. The Himalayan regions of Ladakh and Leh have remained Buddhist since ancient times. His Holiness, the 14th Dalai Lama, leader of Tibetan Buddhism, resides at Dharamsala in western Himachal Pradesh.

Buddhism stands on three pillars: the Buddha, its founder; Dharma, his teachings; and Sangha, the order of monkhood. The essence of Buddhism lies in the Four Noble Truths and the Noble Eightfold Path. The Buddha taught that desire is the root of all suffering and that detachment and freedom from desire can lead to higher wisdom. The Noble Eightfold Path includes right view, thought, speech, action, livelihood, effort, mindfulness, and contemplation. Following this path Buddhists can free themselves of ignorance, control their senses, and attain nirvana, or release from the cycle of births and deaths.

Buddhist monks gathering for Puja at the Mahabodhi Temple in Bodhgaya, Bihar.

Buddhism was divided into three routes to enlightenment after the Buddha's death. Theravada (or Sthaviras; teaching of the elders), the original form, is practiced in India, Burma, Sri Lanka, and Thailand. The easier-to-follow teachings of the Mahayana sect are popular in Tibet, China, Korea, and Japan. Vajrayana is an esoteric offshoot of Mahayana that introduced magic, mysticism, and the worship of male-female union. Japanese Zen is the meditative aspect of Buddhism known as Dhyana.

JAINISM

Jina, meaning "one who has conquered the senses," is the name given to Vardhamana or Mahavira, the great reformer and religious leader who lived in the Buddha's time. Mahavira's followers, known as Jains, practice control of the senses. Although Jainism developed before Buddhism and spread through southern India, it has only about 5 million followers, mainly among the merchant communities of Gujarat, Uttar Pradesh, and Rajasthan.

In the past Jains contributed substantially to India's social and cultural life. Many Hindu practices, such as vegetarianism and fasting, are of Jain origin. Jains adhere to a strict physical and mental discipline. Through a rigorous code of morality, self-denial, and nonviolence, they strive to achieve salvation. To this day orthodox Jains abstain from onions and garlic—said to increase sensual desires—and fermented edibles for fear of harming living bacteria.

Jains and Hindus have merged in several ways: in intermarriage and certain festivals and in the worship of Lakshmi, the goddess of wealth. The Jain symbol is the swastika, auspicious to Hindus and Buddhists.

There are two main sects of Jainism. The Swetambaras worship a Mahavira dressed in a white robe, and the monks and nuns all wear white clothes. The Digambaras worship an unadorned Mahavira, a huge statue of whom stands majestically at Shravanabelagola in Mysore. Because they practice nonattachment to the body, male Digambara monks do not wear any clothes.

SIKHISM

The word *Sikh* is derived from the Sanskrit *shiksha*, which means "to learn." In the Punjabi language it refers to a learner or a disciple. The followers of Guru Nanak and his nine spiritual successors have come to be known as Sikhs. Guru Nanak's sayings and verses are found in the holy book of Guru Granth Sahib, which Sikhs regard in their homes and in *gurdwaras* (gurd-wah-rahs), or Sikh temples. The Sikh religion today has a following of more than 20 million people worldwide.

Guru Nanak, the founding teacher of Sikhism, was born in 1469 in a village called Talwandi Rai Bhoe, now in Pakistan. Guru Nanak was spiritual even as a young boy, rejecting caste and religious distinctions and preaching the doctrine of one God, which he simply called *Ikk* (ache), or One. He felt that God could be perceived through loving devotion.

Sikhism grew into an institution only under the fifth teacher, Guru Arjan Dev, in the 16th century. He constructed the Harimandir, the Golden

A Sikh devotee reading prayers from the Sikh holy book.

Temple at Amritsar, the holiest Sikh shrine today. His successor, Guru Hargobind, adorned himself with two swords and gave a martial direction to Sikhism. Within a century after that, Sikhism became a cohesive social and political force.

Traditional Sikh men are easily identified by the five Ks: *Kesh* (uncut hair since birth, covered by a turban and a beard); *Kara* (steel bangle); *Kachhera* (cotton underwear); *Kanga* (wooden comb); and *Kirpan* (a small sword). However, many modern Sikh men no longer follow these customs.

Sikhs are believed to make good warriors due to a fearless tenacity, indicated by their surname, Singh, which means "lion." Culturally Sikhs are like the Hindus of the Punjab region, and intermarriage used to be common. Since 1980, however, tension and violence between Sikhs and Hindus have been increasing, with an extremist group calling for an independent Sikh homeland, *Khalistan*, meaning "Land of the Pure."

ISLAM

Islam came to India—as it had in almost all countries where it is present today—as a military power led by Muslim conquerors and Arab merchants in the year A.D. 715. Many Hindus converted to Islam. Some were offered economic incentives as a reward, whereas others were drawn by Islam's high ideal of universal brotherhood.

Islam is an Arabic word meaning "submission to Allah" and "peace." Its founder, the Prophet Muhammad, was born in Mecca in the sixth century A.D. Muslims believe that he received divine messages from God and that these messages are collected in the sacred book, the Koran.

All Muslims follow certain basic principles that are enshrined in the Koran. They must profess their faith in Allah, the one ultimate God; recite prayers

Muslim worshipers at the Tippu Sultan Mosque in Kolkata.

five times a day; fast during the month of Ramadan; give a part of their wealth to charity; and go on a hajj (a pilgrimage to Mecca in Saudi Arabia) at least once in their lifetime if they can afford it.

Islam spread throughout India, but the Muslim population today is concentrated in the states of Uttar Pradesh, Bengal, Kashmir, Kerala, Hyderabad, Tamil Nadu, and Gujarat. Indian Muslims work in many sectors of the economy, but most are merchants, artists, and artisans. There are two main Islamic sects: Shia and Sunni. Indian Muslims are mostly Sunni. Some practice Sufism, a mystical doctrine that emphasizes direct communion with God through intuitive knowledge.

CHRISTIANITY

India's Christians belong to several groups and churches. The majority are Catholics. Among them, about 5 million Syrian Christians belong to the Church of Saint Thomas. Saint Thomas is believed to have arrived in Cochin

"Like the rainwater that falls into rivers and joins the mighty ocean, all forms of gods and their worship lead to the same Ultimate Being."
—The Bhagavad Gita

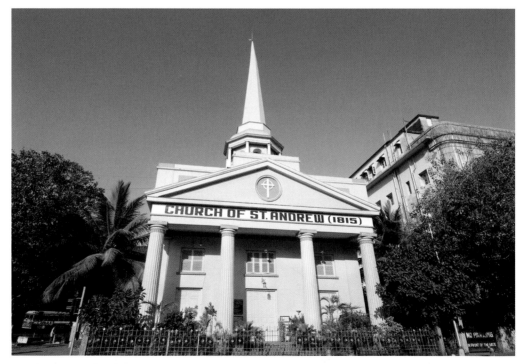

The Church of Saint Andrew in Mumbai.

Mother Teresa was born in 1910 in Skopje, Macedonia (formerly a part of Yugoslavia). In 1950 she founded an order of nuns called the Missionaries of Charity in Kolkata. She gave the rest of her life to caring for the poorest of the poor in India and became known as the Saint of the Gutter. Starting with 12 sisters in India, the Missionaries of Charity has grown to more than 4,000 nuns, running orphanages, AIDS hospices, and other charity centers in 133 countries. Mother Teresa won the Nobel Peace Prize in 1979. She died in 1997.

to spread the message of Jesus Christ in the first century A.D. The arrival of the Portuguese in Goa and the French in Pondicherry in the 16th and 17th centuries brought fresh infusions of Catholicism to these parts.

The history of Protestantism in India commenced with the arrival of two Germans—Bartholomaeus Zieganbalg and Henry Plutschau—in Tranquebar (Tharangambadi) in 1706, with twin objectives: evangelization and Christianization. Marriages between Indians and Europeans also resulted in an ethnic subgroup of Christian Anglo-Indians in this area.

Today there are some 30 million Christians contributing to all sectors of Indian society. Although many Christians who live in the larger cities, such as Mumbai and Kolkata, have adopted Western values and customs, the Christians of southern India, particularly in the suburbs and villages, can hardly be distinguished from their Hindu neighbors, with whom they share many customs and beliefs.

ZOROASTRIANISM

Zoroastrianism takes its name from its founder, Zoroaster, a Persian prophet who pondered life and existence and realized that absolute energy lies in perfect wisdom, which he called Ahura Mazda. His followers are known as Zoroastrians or Parsis (people of Persia). Zoroastrianism is the oldest living religion.

Preceding all other philosophies in India, Zoroastrianism influenced the Indo-Aryan Vedic philosophy in the Vedic period (1500—500 B.C.), although it was only in the 18th century A.D. that a group of Persian Zoroastrians, persecuted by Muslims in their own land, set sail toward Kathiawar and Sanjan in western India and settled there.

Gradually they spread in small colonies, retaining their religious identity but adopting local customs. Afterward they made up an extremely tiny percentage of the Indian population. They were originally farmers, weavers, and toddy-palm planters, but today they are some of India's biggest industrialists.

The holy book of Zend-Avesta contains the founder's sayings, known as *gathas* (gah-thahs). It advocates the worship of Ahu, the source and moving force of life. The luminous sun and the radiant fire are Zoroastrian symbols. The Parsis worship fire in their temples and always have a lighted lamp in their homes.

Parsi moral values stem from the motto, "Good thoughts, good speech, and good deeds lead to perfect wisdom." The ceremonies exclusive to Parsis are Navjoth, the initiation into Zoroastrian ways; *pateti* (pah-tay-ti), the last day of the Zoroastrian calendar; and Navroze, the Parsi New Year. A distinctive feature is the Parsi funeral ceremony, when after prayers they leave the remains of the deceased in the open to be consumed by vultures and crows on top of a high hill, called the Tower of Silence. After a few weeks, when the flesh is completely disintegrated, the bones are then collected and stored in deep wells, whose bottom is covered with charcoal and lime, for dissolution.

TANTRA

Tantra is a spiritual tradition often associated with spells and dark deeds, although this is not a completely accurate view.

Early Tantra followers questioned the supremacy of the Vedas, rejected the Hindu caste system, and dismissed the possibility of life after death. Their desire for prosperity "here and now" brought fertility cults of the mother-goddess into the Tantric fold. With this came the secret art of worshiping the life-giving sexual principle. In the Western world today Tantra is often strongly associated with sex.

Using elaborate diagrams, chants, charms, and hand gestures, the rituals of the Tantra are an attempt to "bring to life" objects of worship. Tantra followers practice yoga, a form of exercise that unites the body with the mind. They look upon the creation of the universe as the blissful union of heaven and earth, spirit and form, and masculine and feminine principles.

Although much of Tantric philosophy has been absorbed into the Hindu religion, some other Tantric practices have been rejected by most Hindus and Tantrists. These activities—black magic performances and the casting of spells to gain control over people—are carried out by obscure groups that often operate in secrecy, headed by leaders who shun public scrutiny.

INTERNET LINKS

www.indiasite.com/religion

This website introduces the main religions in India and describes some important Hindu, Muslim, and Christian places of worship. It also includes articles on Hindu scriptures.

www.hindunet.org

The main focus of this website is the Hindu religion, but it also introduces the main concepts of Jainism, Buddhism, and Sikhism. Of interest are the articles on Hindu gods and a calendar of festivals.

www.motherteresa.org

This official website of the Mother Teresa of Calcutta Center features a biography of the revered nun and the various missions she founded, as well as prayers and testimonies.

LANGUAGE

A man reading the newspaper inside the Karni Mata Temple.

9

A WESTERN SCHOLAR ONCE OBSERVED, "Every Indian district has its own language and customs." There are 600 districts in India, and numerous dialects are spoken in these districts. India's 28 states have been formed not by geopolitical divisions, but rather on the basis of the dominant language spoken in an area.

The Indian constitution has recognized 22 different official languages, in addition to English. The education system favors the study of three

A sign in the gardens of the Viceregal Lodge and Botanical Gardens in Shimla.

The roots of most Indian languages and dialects can be traced back to two main ancient languages: Sanskrit and Pali. There are 22 official languages in India and each has its own written script. In addition to English and Hindi, people are also encouraged to learn their state's own vernacular.

languages in school: Hindi, English, and the vernacular state language. This helps in developing multilingualism, while also promoting the two main official languages.

From ancient times until about the 11th century A.D., there were two dominant language groups in India: the Prakrit languages in the north and the Tamil languages in the south. Pali, adopted by the early Buddhists, was an offshoot of Prakrit, whereas Sanskrit served as the classical literary language of India, much as Latin did in the West. The development of India's languages, each with its own distinct script and literature, was a phenomenon of the medieval period. Sanskrit was increasingly absorbed into the existing vernacular dialects, and philosophical and religious texts were mass-produced in many languages. Thus the vernacular dialects gradually assumed distinct literary styles.

Today the two most widely used language groups are the Indo-Aryan and the Dravidian groups. Sanskrit belongs to the Indo-Aryan group. It is considered to be the ancestor of most Indian languages. Thus, although

A Buddhist mani stone (usually referring to stones with Buddhist prayers inscribed on it) in Ladakh.

"Hindi has always been such a language that it never boycotted any word only because it's of foreign origin."
—Dr. Rajendra Prasad, first president of India

> *Palm leaves and tree bark once served as writing materials, and a sharp iron stylus served as a pen. The stylus inscribed the letters on the leaves, which were smeared with ink to darken the inscription. Excess ink on the leaf surface was wiped away. The bark and leaves were strung together on a cord, so that all holy texts came to be called sutras, or cords.*

Indian languages may appear to be quite different, they do reflect a common culture.

Hindi and its variants are spoken as a mother tongue by more than 40 percent and understood by more than 75 percent of the population.

SCRIPTS

Indian scripts also have a common source. The earliest script, used until the sixth century A.D., for both Tamil and Sanskrit, was Brahmi.

Writing was not, however, the mode of transmitting knowledge in ancient India. Sitting close to the guru, or teacher, the pupil learned verses orally through recitation. Yet, as early as the fourth century B.C., India had not only a well-developed script, but also the greatest of all known Sanskrit grammarians, Panini.

Today all 22 recognized state languages have their own scripts, derived mainly from the Indo-Aryan Sanskrit and the Dravidian Tamil. They are Assamese, Bengali, Bodo, Chhattisgarhi, Dogri, Gujarati, Hindi, Kannada, Kashmiri, Konkani, Malayalam, Manipuri, Marathi, Nepali, Oriya, Punjabi, Sanskrit, Santali, Sindhi, Tamil, Telugu, and Urdu. Urdu, a product of Indo-Muslim fusion, is generally used by the Muslim community.

English, introduced in education in the 19th century, has become a linguistic link for Indians throughout the subcontinent. The language is also an important factor in modernization, though its use is limited to the towns and cities.

TAMIL TRADITION

The only writings that predate the influence of classical Sanskrit are in Tamil. Tamil literature seems to have begun with anthologies of secular lyrics, known as *sangam* (sehng-gehm) poetry. Considered the literary masterpieces of pre-Christian times, they contain some 1,600 verses. Unlike *sangam* poetry (and, incidentally, modern Tamil literature), most traditional Tamil literature is religious in form and content.

In the very early Christian era, a Tamil poet named Tiruvalluvar (who lived in the first century B.C.), wrote beautifully precise moral aphorisms that are still taught to children. The fourth to ninth centuries A.D. saw the growth of intensely rich devotional Tamil poems, forerunners to medieval Indian literature. They were songs in praise of the legendary gods, Shiva, Vishnu, and Krishna. The poet-saints who wrote them were called Alwars and Nayanmars.

Children working on their homework. Besides English, students are encouraged to learn Hindi and their state vernacular language.

The two Tamil romantic epics, *Silapathikaram* and *Manimekalai*, were also composed between the second and fifth centuries A.D. The Tamil version of the Hindu epic *Ramayana* was composed with great eloquence by Kamban, a 10th-century poet.

Tamil literature thereafter went into a deep slumber, perhaps because of political changes. Among modern poets Arunachala Kavi and Subramanya Bharatiyar stand out for their simple and narrative forms of poetry. Mahakkavi Subramania Bharathiar is regarded as one of the greatest Tamil poets, a prolific writer, philosopher, and a great visionary of the 20th century.

SOUTHERN LANGUAGES

The regional languages of southern India include four of India's official languages: Telugu, the state language of Andhra Pradesh; Tamil, the state language of Tamil Nadu; Kannada, the state language of Karnataka;

A newspaper vendor tends to his stall in Mumbai.

A woman practices writing Tamil script.

and Malayalam, the state language of Kerala. The southern languages contain many words from Sanskrit, the court language of many rulers in southern India between the 8th and 15th centuries and have a recorded history of more than 2,000 years.

The greatest Telugu poetry was produced during the time of the Vijayanagara Empire in the 16th century. The king, Krishna Deva Raja, was himself a renowned poet. The 16th and 17th centuries were a golden period for Telugu literature, especially in southern India. Telugu became the language of the south, after Saint Thyagaraja began singing the raga, emotionally charged lyrical verses in classical melodies.

Kannada also produced devotional poetry, the greatest of which was the 10,000-verse ballad, *Bharatesha Vaibhava*, written by the 16th-century poet Ratnakarvarni Varni. Inscriptions in Kannada dating from the sixth century A.D. have been found. Among the earliest literary works are the *Kavirajamarga*, written around 850, and *Lilavati*, a royal love story written in 1370. One of the most famous works is the *Rajasekhara Vilasa*, a morality tale written in 1657 about Shiva's rescue of a royal family from tragedy.

A dialect that has adopted the Kannada script is Tulu, widely spoken in the Malabar region.

Malayalam seems to have existed even earlier than the ninth century. Some of the literature produced in Malayalam suggests a strong Buddhist influence. Apart from mystical verses or *champus* (chahm-poos), Malayalam developed a variety of dramatic literature suited for dance dramas known as Kathakali.

NORTHERN LANGUAGES

Although Prakrit is recognized as the forerunner to the northern Indian languages, it would not be easy for someone who knows one of these languages to understand another without adequate exposure. Every language has produced its own literary masterpieces, some of which have crossed linguistic divisions and become famous throughout India.

Greatest among the vernacular literati was the 20th-century poet, dramatist, and artist, Rabindranath Tagore (1861—1941) of Bengal, who won the Nobel prize for his poetry. He evokes a unique sense of reverence among Indians in general and the Bengalis in particular.

SANSKRIT LITERATURE

The earliest Sanskrit literature, the *Vedas*, probably dates back to 1500 B.C. Since the hymns were passed down orally for several centuries before they were written down, nobody knows their exact origin. The first text, the *Rig Veda*, consists of 1,028 hymns in praise of the gods of nature; the *Sama Veda* is a musical composition of the *Rig Veda*; the *Yajur Veda* is a book of mystical formulas; and the *Atharva Veda* contains magic and charms as medical prescriptions. Believed to be divinely inspired, these four *Vedas* became the repository of all knowledge in India. As Vedic philosophy was difficult to understand, old world legends known as *Puranas* were born. These imaginative tales about gods and goddesses helped the common people understand ethical values. Sanskrit dominated the literary scene for over a thousand years, inspiring the growth of several languages in India and parts of Asia and living up to its epithet, language of the gods.

HINDI

Hindi is a product of several dialects spoken in central and northern India. All of them are folk dialects that trace their roots to Prakrit. Pure Hindi uses a liberal dose of Sanskrit and many Urdu words. Indians regard Hindi as

An Indian man poses for the camera while using his cell phone.

ideal for communication but readily switch to English when it comes to technical subjects.

Several Hindu and Sufi mystics contributed to the enrichment of Hindi in the medieval period. The most outstanding was the 15th-century poet Saint Kabir. His soul-stirring verses, containing a fusion of Hindu and Muslim beliefs, are a landmark in the growth of Hindi.

The greatest Hindi poet to date, however, is the 16th-century saint Goswami Tulsidas, whose devotional epic, *Ram Charit Manas*, retold the *Ramayana* in the language of the masses, making the scripture accessible to the layperson.

Modern Hindi prose began only in the 20th century, with writers such as Mahavir Prasad Dwivedi and Maithili Sharan Gupt.

An offshoot of Hindi is Urdu (a word that means "military camp" in Turkish). Urdu began as a campsite language of Hindu and Muslim soldiers in the Hyderabad region of southern India and then acquired Hindi vocabulary and Arabic script, thus blending languages, thoughts, and beliefs.

Prolific Urdu poets who are appreciated both in India and Pakistan include Mirza Ghalib (1796—1869); the 20th-century poet Mohammed Iqbal; and Bahadur Shah Zafar (1775—1862), the last of the Mughal emperors.

GESTURES AND EXPRESSIONS

India's oral tradition has many gestures, expressions, and proverbs. Greetings among friends invariably invoke a god's name. *Jai Ramji ki* (jye rahm-jee kee), meaning "May Lord Rama be victorious and protect us," is a common greeting in the rural areas in the north, whereas *vanakkam swami* (veh-neh-kehm swah-mi), meaning "I bow to you, divine one," is a welcome in the south.

It is considered respectful to touch the feet of elders or to prostrate oneself before them. The expression when leaving is "I'll go and come back" or "I'll be back," never simply "I'm going." In any Indian dialect, the latter suggests one is leaving this life.

It is common to address any man, whether friend or stranger, as *bhai* (bhye), or "brother," and any woman as *behen* (beh-hane), or "sister." The correct form of address during speeches is *bhaiyo* or *beheno* (bhye-yoh or beh-hane-noh), meaning "brothers and sisters."

An amazing uniformity exists in the oral tradition. Proverbs, such as "one who cannot dance blames the stage or finds fault with the floor" and "a dog's tail can never be straightened," are used in every dialect.

English has greatly influenced language and literature over the last 200 years. Prose literature and blank verse have invaded the literary world. It is now common in India to think in English and speak in the mother tongue or vice versa.

INTERNET LINKS

www.hindilanguage.org

This is a comprehensive website on the Hindi language, detailing its history, literature, and grammar. This site also provides a translation box as well as a list of basic words.

www.Kolkataweb.com/tagore

This site gives a biography of Tagore and a chronology of his works in addition to an English translation of *Gitanjali*, the poet's most famous work. Also featured in this site are some paintings done by Tagore.

www.indianenglishliterature.com

In addition to containing everything about Indian literature in English, this website includes a historical perspective and an alphabetical listing of Indian authors writing in English. This site also showcases reviews and recent works.

ARTS

An elderly Rajput man in traditional dress plays two flutes at once through his nose.

10

A

RT IS A PREOCCUPATION IN INDIA, more an expression of a way of life than a pastime. It reflects India's philosophy, and its origins are as old as the history of the subcontinent. It has grown and developed at different levels to serve different functions.

Whether it is jewelry beaten out of metal, delicate woven shawls and brocade saris, or carved wood and stone, few other nations have so exuberant a variety of arts.

The Indian performing arts do not have well-defined categories, such as the Western forms of opera, ballet, dance, or drama. Very often they are an interesting blend of all these forms. Folk, ritual, and classical elements exist side by side, influencing one another.

Yet broad classifications of the Indian arts are possible according to region, style, and purpose. The folk arts, for instance, may be connected with social revelry to celebrate successful hunting, fishing, or harvesting. The ritual or ceremonial arts are generally of the mystical variety,

Right: Stick dancers performing during the annual Elephant Festival.

Art is an integral part of Indian culture, from its ancient stories like the *Ramayana*, to its folk art, music, classical dances, and even its famous Bollywood films.

performed in temples as fertility rites. The classical arts of dance and music are highly stylized and refined and require years of training and academic scholarship.

Whatever the style or form, Indian arts convey a single theme: *rasa* (rah-sah), the essence of the joy of life. All Indian arts fuse with religious devotion, and this applies equally to music, dance, drama, poetry, painting, sculpture, and handicrafts.

Monks in elaborate and beautiful costumes performing during a monastery festival.

FOLK ART

Whether it is to celebrate spring or the monsoon season, the birthday of a mythic god, or the installation of a deity, festival time in rural India means adorning the village cows, elephants, and camels and decorating streets and homes with folk motifs symbolizing prosperity and abundance. The nights are filled with singing and dancing, and tales of gods and goddesses are played out.

Each region has its own style and form of dance. Punjab is famous for its rugged Bhangra, whereas Gujarat is known for its gentler Garba and Raas dances. The southern Indian street dances are called Therukkuthu, whereas Kavadi and Karagam are more ritualistic dances performed by devotees as wish-fulfilling prayers.

Community dances—such as the Lama dances of the Himalayan region and the Chhau dance of eastern India—may involve magic, sorcery, or religious ritual. The Theyyattam dance of north Kerala incorporates drama into rhythm and movement for fuller expression. To the music of powerful percussion instruments, the dancers re-create awesome characters in myths depicting the victory of good over evil.

"Tabla belongs to that rare breed of percussion that developed only in India."
—Dr. Ragini Trivedi, sitar player

POETRY

All classical Indian art forms can be traced back to poetry. The recitation of the Vedas is believed to have given rise to musical notes and scales. To this day it is poetry that is rendered as classical music. Classical dance too captures the poet's innermost feelings through mime and hand gestures. Dance is thought of as visual poetry, sculpture as frozen poetry.

An intricate frieze depicting a scene from the *Mahabharata* at the Kailasa Temple.

In fact most ancient works—fables, epic tales, and mathematical, scientific, and philosophical works—were composed in poetic form. Verse, with the rhyme and regular meter, was easier to memorize and transmit orally. Prose is a comparatively recent phenomenon.

Apart from the abundant religious literature in India—especially the *Mahabharata* and the *Ramayana*—Kalidasa's *Shakkuntalam* in Sanskrit and Ilango Adigal's *Silappadhikaram* in Tamil are among the famous secular works of ancient India. In modern times Ayyappa Paniker's *Kurukshetram* is considered a Malayalam masterpiece and has been translated into other languages, including Hindi, French, and English.

The 1930s nurtured a new generation of poets. The progressive poets drew inspiration from Karl Marx, the most influential socialist thinker of the 19th century, and focused on the themes of political and social revolution in their poems. They concentrated on ideas and ideology rather than aesthetics and forms of expression. The most prominent of the progressive writers was Faiz Ahmed Faiz, who succeeded in blending ideas and aesthetics in his poems.

Contact with Islamic culture, beginning in the early eighth century, brought a fusion of Indian and Muslim thought, as reflected in the *thumri* (thoom-ri) and *ghazal* (gheh-zehl), or love poetry. The *ghazal* is a short poem made up of couplets, each a complete idea in itself. The first couplet sets the tone of the poem, and the last couplet usually expresses a personal thought or intent, such as a prayer for a loved one.

MUSIC

Classical Indian music is spiritual in character. Sound is believed to have originated as a divine gift of the Lord of all Creation, Brahma. From this mystical origin, classical Indian music developed into a complex system as early as the second century A.D. Temples served as places of learning and performing. Gods and goddesses provided the theme.

When Muslim rulers introduced music in their courts, romantic and secular music began to evolve with Persian and central Asian elements. This gave rise to two distinct styles of music: the northern Hindustani and the southern Karnatak.

Both styles are based on the system of raga, which means "color" or "mood." A raga is a melodic base with characteristic ascending and descending notes. It conveys a mood or an emotion. In fact there is a raga for every occasion—even for every part of the day! The individual performer interprets a melody to produce hours of improvised music. This is what makes Indian music unique.

Indian music follows a rhythm cycle known as tala. Complex rhythmic patterns are woven in, and improvisation is allowed. In a classical music ensemble, a percussion instrument to mark the beat and a violin or a *sarangi* (sah-REHNG-gi)—a string instrument played with a bow—provide the accompaniment.

Music students learn by oral demonstration by their guru, and much is learned through attentive listening and years of practice. Traditionally students live with their guru and absorb the master's technique.

A Rajasthani man playing the *sarangi*, a traditional Indian stringed instrument.

MUSICAL INSTRUMENTS

There are about 500 different kinds of Indian musical instruments, each with a distinct shape and tone. Many are indigenous, some are of foreign origin, and a few are ingenious adaptations. Most can be classified as string, wind, or percussion instruments.

The most ancient of these instruments are the drums and gongs. The name for the southern Indian percussion, *mridangam* (body of clay), suggests its primitive beginnings. The highly refined modern mridangam is capable of producing a wide variety of sounds. In the north the tabla, a two-piece drum possibly derived from the Arabic tabla, constitutes a vital part of Indian music today.

String instruments are of the bowing, plucking, and striking kind. The simplest of all is the one-string *ektara* (drone) that the singing bards carry. The *veena*, popular in the south today, was prevalent even in King Ashoka's time (third century B.C.).

The sitar, made popular by the famous classical music genius, Ravi Shankar, is derived from the Persian *sehtar* and adapted by the 13th-century court poet, Amir Khusrau. The *sarod* evolved from Afghanistan's *rebab*, whereas the Western violin has found a permanent place among classic Indian instruments.

Wind instruments include the bamboo flute and the reed-piped *nadaswaram* and *shehnai*. None of these have metallic keys like their Western counterparts do. Clever manipulation of the stops or finger holes is required.

Musicians performing at Shilpgram village.

CLASSICAL DANCE

Classical dance in India is based on standards laid down by the sage Bharatha more than 2,000 years ago. They pertain to footwork, gestures, facial expressions, dress, and makeup. Five regional styles have evolved based on these forms.

The southern *Bharatha Natyam* (bhah-rah-tah-NEHT-yehm) is one of the most popular forms. Dancers in elaborate costume, jewelry, and hairdos perform intricate footwork in a half-seated posture. Hand gestures and facial expressions narrate mythic, heroic, or romantic tales. One dancer enacts all the roles, switching from emotion to emotion—joy, anger, mirth, fear, anguish, sorrow, and so on.

Kathakali (kehth-keh-li) is the mimetic or mime-like dance of Kerala. With huge headdresses and heavily painted faces, men enact supernatural roles, often both male and female. Powerful percussion instruments accompany this outdoor dance, usually performed in the temple courtyard.

Odissi (oh-DIS-si), the dance form of eastern India, is flowing and sensuous, reminding one of the beautiful sculptures of the Konarak temple in Orissa. *Manipuri* is another eastern dance, the subtle movements of which resemble Burmese, Thai, and Cambodian dances.

Kathak (keh-thek) is the northern form, which emphasizes footwork and swift, swirling pirouettes. Having entered the royal courts of the Muslim kings in the medieval period, *Kathak* has assimilated other cultural influences. *Kuchipudi* and *Mohiniattam* are neoclassical dances of the south, with strong folk elements in their music and gestures.

Uday Shankar, Rukmini Devi, and Balasaraswati are three of the best-known Indian classical dancers.

THEATER

Traditional Indian theater is more like a dance drama; it is very different from the dialogue-based Western drama. Rural regions have a whole array of folk forms such as musical opera, masked theater, and puppetry. Generally, in Indian theater, a narrator links up plots and subplots, and a clown provides humor in between. The rest of the cast is broadly classified as good or bad characters.

With a simple orchestra, a temporarily constructed wooden stage, and elaborate dress and makeup, actors and actresses entertain the villagers from dusk to dawn on festive occasions. Regional styles may vary, but the themes are generally from old world legends: the *Puranas*, the *Ramayana*, and the *Mahabharata*.

In the past a whole social class of performers grew out of the theatrical tradition. *Chakyars* or *bhagavatars* in the south, originally of the Brahman caste, took to entertaining to teach the people moral values. The art of storytelling was taken up by *bhanas* (bhah-nahs), the singing minstrels. Only temple dancers, known as *devadasis* (they-vah-thah-sees), were considered socially inferior. The *devadasi* system was later outlawed because of exploitation by wealthy patrons.

Modern Indian plays are quite like plays performed on a Western stage; mythical themes are replaced by social themes, and dialogue dominates the show. Mumbai and Bengal produce plays that are a blend of Western and Indian theater.

Unfortunately movies and television are fast replacing the stage in many rural and urban places. However, the *Ramayana* and the *Mahabharata* have made a dramatic comeback in the form of television serials—old themes in a new medium.

Rajasthani puppets for sale. The rising popularity and accessibility of television and film has seen a decline in performances such as theater and puppetry.

ARCHITECTURE

India is full of artistic legacies from the past. One of the most obvious is Indian architecture, which is a tapestry of buildings incorporating many art forms. Some are in total ruin, whereas others remain astonishingly intact. The southern Hindu temples are architectural masterpieces, and the Hoysala temples at Habebid in Mysore have been described as a "stone lacework of moving magnificence."

The Ellora Caves in Aurangabad boasts an architectural marvel. There craftsmen once excavated huge mountain rocks, carved the walls into powerful pillars and statues, chiseled out the interior to fill it with amazing frescoes, and then carved a series of chapels and monasteries deep into the rock. These are known as the Kailasha Temple, the mountain abode of Lord Shiva.

In the medieval period many temples in the north were razed to make way for mosques, minarets, and tombs. The 238-foot (72.5-m) Qutub Minar, the Jama Masjid or Pearl Mosque, and the tombs scattered all over the old city of Delhi testify to this transformation. Elsewhere slender minarets and spired domes with intricate inlays are reminders of Indo-Muslim art.

The British gave India the imposing Gateway of India in Mumbai and the Victorian-style palace of the viceroy in New Delhi. Today the latter is known as the Rashtrapati Bhavan and serves as the official residence of the president of India. Some of the universities, churches, and libraries in Mumbai, Chennai, and Kolkata were built during India's colonial era.

Buildings in Pondicherry are distinctly French in structure, whereas those in Goa, near Mumbai, display a strong Portuguese influence.

The Kailasa Temple in Ellora.

THE MOST BEAUTIFUL BUILDING IN THE WORLD

The Taj Mahal is the most perfect example of Mughal architecture. Built entirely of white marble, it glows in the light of the full moon and takes on the colors of the sun at dawn and dusk. Starting in A.D. 1631, it took 20,000 of the finest artisans from India and Central Asia and 22 years to complete this 42-acre (17-ha) enchanting marble mausoleum on the banks of the Yamuna River. In all 28 types of rare, semiprecious, and precious stones were used for embellishing the Taj Mahal. The mausoleum is covered with arabesque designs, making for a perfect symmetry of architectural elements, and the gardens fronting the Taj reflect this geometric pattern. The walls and ceilings are decorated with calligraphy and motifs of flowers inlaid with precious stones such as agate and jasper.

In 1983 the Taj Mahal was designated a World Heritage Site by UNESCO and it is one of the most visited places in India.

INTERNET LINKS

www.artindia.net

This website provides an authentic treasure trove of information on classical Indian dance and music. The site also features articles on a number of other artistic expressions.

www.kattaikkuttu.org

This site is devoted to *kataikkuttu*, a theatrical art form of Tamil Nadu. The website explains the characteristics of the genre and describes how the plays are performed. Additionally the site includes a list of plays in the repertoire.

www.arts.indianetzone.com

This site is a comprehensive resource on Indian arts, including crafts, photography, and festivals, in addition to classical dance and art.

LEISURE

A girl playing on a swing.

11

LIFE MOVES AT A SEDATE PACE IN India, and Indians make the time for recreation and entertainment. In the cities, however, the pace can get quite hectic for working adults, even though they make it a point to attend family activities.

People in the countryside revel in outdoor games; indoor games such as chess, parcheesi, and five stones; street shows and other traditional pastimes; and competitive games such as racing, wrestling, and *kabaddi* (kah-bah-di), a team game that requires skillful breathing and dodging.

In the cities most of the games introduced by the British are popular. Generally the Bengalis prefer soccer, the Punjabis prefer hockey, and the residents of Mumbai prefer cricket. In the mountainous regions, climbing, hiking, and skiing are seasonal sports, whereas in the coastal regions, swimming, fishing, and boat-racing are the obvious favorites.

In the world of entertainment, India is known for its traditional storytellers—the bardic

Right: Boys playing cricket. Cricket is one of the most popular sports in India.

THE *RAMAYANA*

Once there lived a king named Dasharatha, who had three wives and four sons. His eldest son, Rama, was exiled for 14 years, just when he was about to be crowned, because the king was bound by promises he had made to his youngest queen. When Rama was in the forest with his wife Sita and brother Lakshmana, a wicked and lustful king, Ravana, came in the guise of a sage and abducted Sita. Rama and Lakshmana, with the help of the monkey god Hanuman, went in search of Sita. They killed Ravana and his mighty army, and Rama returned to rule. In this tale, Rama stands for righteous duty, Sita for purity and truth, and Ravana for arrogance and greed. The Ramayana *is a living tradition in India and other parts of Asia.*

folk singers of the north or the *bhagavatars* of the south—who weave tales with songs and mimicry, holding their listeners' attention for hours. Some of these storytellers even double as puppeteers to re-create myths and legends.

STORYTELLING

The bhagavatars sing their tales in temples, infusing them with religious and moral values. The *Ramayana* and the *Mahabharata*, which highlight the triumph of the righteous over the wicked, are of eternal interest.

However, the movie theater has become the most popular form of entertainment, and television has invaded even the most remote villages. Film heroes and heroines have cashed in on mass adulation, and some have even taken on new roles in politics.

TRADITIONAL PASTIMES

Many wooden and clay dolls in India resemble Hindu gods and goddesses, because they have been shaped by the same artisans who produce holy images for religious use. Girls in India usually play jump rope, or hopscotch, and five stones, tossing the stones up in the air and catching them in many different ways. The swing is so popular in India that homes in the south have permanent swings installed in their yards. In the north women celebrate a festival called Teej, when tall swings are set up amid groves of trees for young and old to swing in and sing praises of the monsoon season.

Organized sporting events are usually a feature of festivals. In the colorful harvest festival of Onam in Kerala, in the months of August and September, beautifully decorated boat processions culminate in exciting snakeboat races. Snakeboats, known as *chundam vallam*, are like large kayaks that can fit over 90 paddlers. The boats are about 6 feet (1.8 m) wide and about 196—213 feet (60—65 m) long, with a curl at its stern.

The harvest festivals of Tamil Nadu feature bullock races and bullfighting competitions, whereas camel races and polo take center stage in the desert festivals of Rajasthan. Then there are the coconut-plucking contests, groundnut-eating races, and even bride-winning feats of rural India. However, at the top of the list is the traveling circus. Folks travel from the villages by the busload, when the circus comes to town.

Snake boats preparing for a race on the Pampa River.

GAMES FROM THE PAST

Since ancient times Indians have been known to spend hours playing board games: archaeological digs have unearthed stone and ivory dice. Gambling and bullfighting are believed to have been introduced in southern India by Roman seafarers, whereas archery and hunting were the preserve of royalty in Vedic times.

A man stretches before his morning yoga exercises overlooking the Ganges River.

Chess is known to have originated in ancient India, from where the game spread to West and Southeast Asia. The Malay tiger game has its origin in the southern Indian game of *puli kattu* (poo-li kaht-too), a board game played with three tigers to a dozen goats, represented by stones and shells. To score, the goats—represented by stones—must completely encircle each tiger—represented by a shell.

Parcheesi is a common indoor game in the villages. There is a parcheesi gameboard carved on the wall of the fifth-century temple on Elephanta Island near Mumbai. The game was so popular with the Mughal Emperor Akbar that he ordered parcheesi squares to be cut in the pavement of his palace quadrangle and used his slaves as living pieces.

Akbar also introduced polo from Persia to northern India, from where the sport spread to England in the 19th century. Polo is still played in northwestern India and in the Himalayan regions.

Thanks to India's wildlife protection policy, as tiger and lion hunting—popular in the medieval period, especially among the maharajas (meaning "king")—has been replaced by a less cruel form of hunting: shooting with a camera.

KABADDI AND YOGA

Two outdoor games that are distinctly Indian and require considerable skill are *kabaddi* and *kho-kho* (khoh-khoh). Kabaddi requires neither elaborate equipment nor a sports arena. Any number of people, organized in two teams, can play this simple game of breath control.

A line is drawn on the ground, and the teams gather on either side. A player from one team runs into the opposing team's side. He shouts "*kabaddi*" or "hu-tu-tu" repeatedly without stopping to breathe and tries to touch a member of the opposing team and run back to his own team before his breath runs out. The opposing team's members try to dodge the intruder. But if one of them is hit, they band together to try to keep the intruder away from his team. If the intruder manages to reunite with his team before running out of breath, his team scores a point. Otherwise the opposing team scores.

A great part of the fun in *kabaddi* is crowd participation. Spectators cheer and jeer, and some bet heavily on the outcome as the match gathers momentum.

Although *kabaddi* is played mainly by men, *kho-kho* can be played by men, women, and children of all ages. This catching game played by two teams has also become one of India's national games.

Learning to control the mind and body is the object of yoga and the martial arts of *kalari payat* (kah-lah-ri pah-yat). Some schools teach yoga to help children build supple bodies and a sharp intellect. Health-conscious city folk take morning walks and practice yoga in gardens and parks.

Sachin Tendulkar of India is lifted by his teammates during the lap of honor after India's victory over Sri Lanka in the International Cricket Council World Cup Final in 2011.

MODERN SPORTS

India is progressing in the world of sports. Good facilities have been provided for sportsmen and sportswomen, games are promoted, and grants are awarded to the skilled and talented.

A Bollywood movie poster in New Delhi.

Soccer, basketball, cricket, field hockey, and volleyball are popular group sports in urban India. Elite clubs offer tennis, badminton, squash, golf, and billiards. Skiing, skating, vintage car rallies, and yachting are rising recreational activities among the affluent.

Closest to the heart for most Indians is cricket. When the national team plays test matches, people tune in to radios blaring the running commentary. Important matches are broadcast live on TV and cricket means big business in India, with celebrity players attaining star status. The most fiercely contested games are those that pit Indian teams against their archrival, Pakistan.

India pioneered the Asian Games, held for the first time in New Delhi (India) in March 1951. When the 9th Asian Games returned to New Delhi in 1982, more than 30 countries were represented by about 5,000 participants in the spectacular event. In 2010 India hosted the Commonwealth Games, a sporting event that attracted more than 7,000 athletes from 71 countries belonging to the British Commonwealth. The games proved to be a valuable showcase for Indian sports as well as its infrastructure and hospitality.

INDIAN CINEMA

While the term *Bollywood* has become synonymous with Indian cinema, it in fact only refers to Hindi-language films. There are many other Indian films that are produced in the various Indian languages—for instance, Tamil, Gujarati, and Bengali films. Expatriate Indian communities in other Asian countries as well as in the United States and the United Kingdom have helped bring Indian cinema to the world and boost its popularity.

India is the world's larger producer of films, producing 1,288 feature films in 2009.

BOLLYWOOD is probably best known for its colorful costumes, catchy songs, and dances. However, the Golden Age of Hindi Cinema is thought to be around the 1940s to 1960s, after the independence of India. Some of the greatest Bollywood films, such as *Pyaasa* (1957), were produced during this time. The themes of Bollywood films have evolved over time, from mainly romance and melodrama to gangsterism and violence. However, romance still remains a popular theme today. With their increased presence in the Western world, many Bollywood films now include more English dialogue, and many films are set in locations outside of India. Films such as *Moulin Rouge* and *Slumdog Millionaire* are said to have drawn direct inspiration from Bollywood.

INTERNET LINKS

www.nriol.com/indianparents/indian-games.asp

This website provides detailed explanations on some typical Indian games. It gives the history of the games as well as the rules that govern them.

www.bcci.tv

This official website of the Board of Control for Cricket in India gives a detailed history of the game in India. The site features the national teams as well as news and interviews with players and officials. Of special interest to the cricket fan are the list of fixtures and results of matches.

www.bestindianfilms.com

In addition to features on Bollywood (its history, music, and dance), this website gives a rundown on the other locales of the Indian movie industry as well as movie reviews and insights on famous actors.

FESTIVALS

Elephants at a Hindu temple festival in Kerala.

12

FESTIVALS ARE A colorful expression of Indian traditions: of changing seasons and harvesting cycles, of Vedic myths and legends, of social and spiritual renewal.

Indian festivals are bewilderingly diverse. Most of them have a religious character, some being an interesting fusion of Hindu-Buddhist, Hindu-Muslim, or Hindu-Christian beliefs. Some are national, secular events, such as Republic Day and Independence Day. Many are confined to specific regions and religions, while a few are celebrated only by certain castes and clans.

With more than six religions celebrating the birthdays of gods and saints, Indians have a multitude of occasions to celebrate. In fact there is some form of social revelry or temple festivity almost every other day of the year. Hindu festival dates are fixed by the Indian calendar, which follows the lunar cycle and corresponds with the agricultural cycle of sowing and reaping.

Festivals in the villages are invariably accompanied by fairs and cultural performances that may go on for a week to 10 days. Often plants and animals also have a place in the celebrations, and on at least one occasion, even the spirits of the dead are invited. Hindu festivals often begin with fasting and end with feasting; disciplined abstinence is a prelude to joyous abandon.

COMMON FESTIVALS

The Hindu New Year is celebrated in India sometime in the month of Chaitra (mid-March to mid-April). It is called Gudi

Festivals in India are loud and colorful affairs. Religious and national holidays are both celebrated with equal pomp.

Right: A painted elephant walks down the street during the Gangaur festival.

117

Padwa in Maharashtra, Nav Warih in Kashmir, and Varuda Pirappu in Tamil Nadu. The date and method of celebration vary from place to place. Usually singing and dancing culminate in a visit to a temple.

The second lunar month (April—May)—known as Vaishakha (Vaisakhi or Vesak)—is auspicious to Hindus, Buddhists, and Sikhs. The full moon day of Vaishakha is associated with the Buddha's birth, enlightenment, and nirvana (release from the cycle of births and deaths). Interestingly the Hindus regard it as the birth month of Shiva's son, Kartikeya, who also grants enlightenment to his worshipers on this day. Buddhists form a procession led by an image of the Buddha riding a chariot drawn by four horses. The devotees go around the temple, prostrating themselves and chanting, offering prayers and lighting candles at the altar, releasing caged animals, and performing acts of charity.

The first new moon day of April to May is the birth anniversary of Guru Hargobind, the founder of the Sikh movement Khalsa. The Sikh New Year, known as Vaisakhi, is primarily a social occasion when the traditional Bhangra is danced all through the night. Punjabi villagers dress colorfully, take part in processions, drink, and sing joyfully.

FAMILY FESTIVALS

Although there is no Father's Day, Mother's Day, or Senior Citizen's Day in India, there are many festivals that celebrate family relationships.

In the north, during the festival of Raksha Bandhan on the full moon in July to August, a girl ties a decorated silk thread around her brother's wrist and applies a dot of vermilion powder on his forehead. She makes sweets for him as a symbol of her affection. Her brother in turn gives her gifts and promises to protect her all his life, thus strengthening the sibling bond.

A festival called Karva Chauth in the north and Karadayan Nonbu in the south is celebrated sometime in October or November to strengthen affection between married couples. The wife prays for the husband's well-being and fasts for a day, at the end of which she is blessed with a happy married life.

Pitrupaksh or Shraddha is a ceremony devoted to ancestors. The spirits are believed to descend upon earth to participate in the ceremony sometime

"Let this Diwali burn all your bad times and enter you in good times."
—Popular Diwali saying

in the first two weeks of September. Food and prayers are offered to crows, which represent the spirits of the dead. Some Indians observe this ceremony on the death anniversary of their relatives.

At around the same time Muslims celebrate Shab-e-Barat, a day when Allah is believed to register a person's actions and dispense his or her fate accordingly. It is an occasion for prayer, fasting, acts of charity, visits to family graves, and offerings of flowers, all of which are followed by feasting and merrymaking.

FESTIVAL MYTHS AND LEGENDS

Every Hindu festival is associated with a mythological tale. The northern festival of Raksha Bandhan recalls the legend of Lord Indra's defeat of the devil. When Indra was fighting a losing battle against the devil, his wife, Indrani, tied a sacred thread around his wrist. With the power of the thread, Indra won the battle.

Dussehra, also called Durga Puja, commemorates the defeat of a demon king by the goddess Durga. Legend has it that the buffalo-headed demon, Mahisasura, became insolent with power and brought pain and suffering on the pious and innocent. Angered by his arrogance, the Hindu Trinity, Brahman, created Durga, a deity with 1,000 arms. Mounted on a lion and armed with Shiva's trident, Vishnu's discus, and Brahma's thunderbolt, Durga conquered the demon.

In West Bengal huge images of Durga are installed in public places for nine days, and then carried by processions of devotees to rivers and lakes for immersion in the water. In Gujarat women sing and dance the traditional Garba and Raas around images of the deity. In Uttar Pradesh and Delhi, the story of Ramayana is reenacted in street performances, and on the 10th day, giant effigies of the 10-headed king, Ravana, and his brothers are burned, symbolizing the victory of righteousness.

In the south the same festival is known as the Doll's Festival. Women arrange images of deities and dolls on a platform in their homes and invite their female friends over, giving them coconuts, betel leaves, turmeric, and vermilion powder as symbols of fertility and prosperity.

A reconstruction of the goddess Durga, a deity created to kill the demon Mahisasura.

People throwing colored powder at one another during the Holi Festival.

DIWALI AND HOLI

Diwali or Deepavali, the festival of lights, is India's most popular festival. It is believed that Lord Krishna killed the demon king, Narakasura, on this dark night. According to another belief, Diwali celebrates Lakshmi, the goddess of wealth and prosperity, who blesses the homes and offices of her devotees on this auspicious day. Whichever the legend, it is a day when the whole of India unrestrainedly rejoices.

Homes, shops, and buildings are cleaned and beautifully decorated with rows of lamps and candles. Several days prior to the festival, people start making sweet dishes and buying new clothes and jewelry for the occasion. Many devotees visit the temple, and the young seek the blessings of the elders. At nightfall oil lamps are lit, turning whole neighborhoods into fairyland. Fireworks are the main attraction for children and adults alike.

The spring festival of the north, popularly known as Holi, is also replete with color, fun, and gaiety. According to legend Holika, the wicked aunt of the divine child Prahlada, decided to burn the boy as punishment for uttering the name of God in vain. Amazingly enough, the fire protected the child and burned his cruel aunt instead!

Huge bonfires are lit on the eve of Holi to mark the destruction of evil. Since Holi is also the water sport played by Lord Krishna and his milkmaids, the streets are full of people throwing colored water and powder at each other with glee. People also visit friends and eat lots of sweets.

GODS' AND SAINTS' BIRTHDAYS

India celebrates the birthdays of gods, saints, gurus, and prophets grandly. In the villages even local heroes receive honor fit for the gods.

"Lead me from the unreal to the real. Lead me from the darkness to light. Lead me from death to immortality."
—An invocation from the Upanishads, the last part of the Vedas

Lord Rama's birthday is a grand affair in temples dedicated to him, but it takes on a special significance in his birthplace, Ayodhya. On Krishna's birthday vignettes from his life unfold in homes, temples, and cultural centers, and children dress up as Krishna and indulge in the naughty acts described in legendary tales of the god's childhood.

Christians celebrate the birth of Jesus Christ. They flock to church at midnight on Christmas Eve or on Christmas morning to attend Mass and see a reenactment of the Nativity. In the cities even the non-Christians put up Christmas trees, exchange gifts, and hold Christmas parties.

Muslims gather at mosques on the Prophet Muhammad's birthday, Milad-un-Nabi, in the third month of the Islamic calendar. This day is marked by special religious discourses and the distribution of alms to the poor.

Sikhs celebrate Guru Purab to mark the birthday of their founder, Guru Nanak. Jains flock to the ancient Jain shrine at Girnar in Gujarat on Mahavira's birthday. Parsis celebrate Khordad Saal, the prophet Zoroaster's birthday, in their temples.

Figurines of the Three Wise Men on sale at a market in Goa during Christmas.

VILLAGE FAIRS

Fairs are an integral part of festivities in India, whatever the sect or religion. Residents of neighboring villages, dressed in all their finery, arrive at village fairs on camels, in bullock carts, on bicycles, and on foot. Hectic buying, bargaining, and selling are the order of the day. Products ranging from kitchen utensils, trinkets, and fresh vegetables to cows and horses are bought and sold. It is also the ideal time for selecting brides and grooms! Magic shows, street dances, puppet theater, folk music, circus shows, and impromptu acts add to the festive spirit of these fairs.

Elephant rides and camel races are common at the Teej and Pushkar fairs in Rajasthan. Bullfighting is a regular feature on the day following the harvest festival of Pongal (mid-January) in the south. Cockfights, and

An aerial view of the fairgrounds of the Pushkar Camel Fair.

the accompanying heavy betting, are also common then. Boat races are popular with the seafarers and fishermen of Kerala during the festival of Onam.

In mountainous Ladakh the annual fair at the beginning of spring includes a ritual performance in Buddhist monasteries. The actors and musicians are lamas or monks, who blow huge trumpets, clap cymbals, and beat drums. Masked figures, gorgeously attired in silk robes, represent spirits and demons. The victory of good and the defeat of the demons are reenacted with stunning effect.

Jains hold a *rathyatra* fair in Meerut in the north to celebrate the birth of three of their saints, called Tirthankaras. The full moon day in October to November sees more than 1 million Jains flocking to the fair.

TESTS OF FAITH

Firewalking is a common test of faith in many rural communities in India. Once a year in the south, firewalking serves as a wish-fulfilling ritual performed in honor of local deities or to ensure a good harvest. Brave Hindu youths bathe in the temple complex, smear their bodies with turmeric, and walk over a bed of live coals.

Muslims, especially the Shias, commemorate the martyrdom of Imam Husain, the grandson of the Prophet Muhammad, with a month of fasting and prayers. Known as Muharram the first month of the Islamic calendar is a solemn period observed with great fervor especially in Lucknow, where, watched by thousands, bands of men walk on beds of live coals. Some even lash themselves with whips in a show of grief.

The Goan festival of Zatra celebrates the visit of the three kings to Bethlehem, where Jesus Christ was born. Three young men dressed as the three kings walk up to a church that shelters a sculpture of the holy infant Jesus. The actors' entrance into the church kicks off feasting and dancing, firewalking and fire-eating.

In January pious devotees of the god Ayyappan abstain from meat, alcohol, and sex, impose other forms of severe discipline on themselves, and walk barefoot several miles up the hill of Sabarimalai in the south.

INTERNET LINKS

www.festivalsofindia.in

This website includes various listings of all the festivals, fairs, and melas in India. All festivals are explored in detail in addition to pages on Hindu gods and goddesses as well as links to other religions.

www.pilgrimage-india.com

Hindu pilgrimage sites are listed by region, and a list of Buddhist pilgrimage sites is provided at this website. It also features details of festivals and fairs as well as articles on Hinduism, Buddhism, and Jainism.

www.pushkar-camel-fair.com

A detailed description of the annual Pushkar Fair in Rajasthan is given at this website. The site also provides articles on the city of Pushkar as well as Pushkar Lake and the temples around the area.

FOOD

Spices on sale at Mapusa Market. Indian cuisine utilizes many different types of spices.

13

"YOU ARE WHAT YOU EAT," especially in India, where food is considered as sacred as the human body. Indians look for balanced nourishment of both body and mind, in the belief that what they eat influences their behavior, attitudes, and well-being.

Spices, milk and milk products, meat, lentils, and vegetables are used in varying amounts, depending on the season, month, or day. All foods have been classified by an ancient science into heating and cooling

An assortment of dried fruits and nuts for sale.

Indian cuisine is complex and diverse. A wide variety of spices, nuts, and fruits are used in cooking. Hindus do not eat beef and many are also vegetarian. Muslims, on the other hand, do not consume pork and only eat food that has been certified as halal.

agents. Indians believe, for instance, that mangoes produce heat, whereas milk and yogurt cool the body. Children are generally given a glass of milk after they eat mangoes to prevent boils and sores in the heat of summer—and it seems to work!

Each food item is believed to possess certain qualities that are transmitted to the consumer. Meat, alcohol, and highly fermented foods are considered base foods that contribute to laziness and greed. Rich and oily foods that have excess spice or sugar are considered royal foods that produce a quick temper and a love of luxury. Indians who wish to calm the body and sharpen the mind generally live on a diet of milk and milk products, fresh fruits and vegetables, lentils, nuts, and grains.

Such food values have considerably influenced the daily diet and eating habits of most Indians.

FOOD VARIETIES

Indian cuisine is as rich and colorful as the country itself. Every region has its own food specialties, although there is a standard Indian meal, consisting of vegetables, meat or fish, a grain, some yogurt, and lentils, or dal.

A man making naan in Ladakh. Naan is a staple that features in most meals.

Depending on the region, the grain could be rice or an Indian wheat bread, such as chapati, puri, naan, or *paratha* (peh-rah-thah). In many middle-class homes, both chapati and rice, often spiced and garnished with vegetables and nuts, are served. However, a poor man's diet might only consist of rice porridge or plain bread with raw onions and green chili.

Lentils are a major source of protein for Indians, and India produces a wide variety of split peas and beans. Lentils are generally eaten daily, and many spices are used to create a range of flavored lentil dishes.

Naan being cooked in a tandoor oven.

Vegetables in season, including gourds, greens, and root vegetables, are popular throughout India. Banana curries and pumpkin with a liberal dash of freshly grated coconut are typical in the south, whereas a dish of green peppers and cauliflower in onion, garlic, and tomato sauce is popular in the north.

Egg and chicken are commonly eaten throughout India; fish and shrimp are hot favorites in the coastal regions.

Islamic influence shows in royal Mughal-style recipes. The cylindrical earthen oven called tandoor has added a spread of oven-baked tandoori breads, such as naan, and tandoori meats, such as chicken and mutton, to the Indian menu.

HABITS AND PRACTICES

Generally Indians rinse their hands, legs, and face before a meal, at which they sit on the floor and eat with their fingers. Among Hindus food is first

"In India, rice is often called 'Prana'—the breath of life."
—Vandana Shiva, environmental activist and ecofeminist

offered to the gods and then served to the family by the woman of the house, who eats only when everyone else has finished.

Indians usually use stainless steel or brass vessels and plates. The wealthy use silver plates; the poorer place their food portions on rectangular sections of banana leaves. In many urban homes partakers of a meal sit at a dining table and use Western-style cutlery.

A traditional Bengali meal takes hours to prepare and is consumed at a leisurely pace. Each person sits on a small carpet on the floor. A large steel platter or piece of fresh-cut banana leaf lying in front of the carpet presents hot rice with lime wedges, whole green chilies, and a little pickle. Small metal or earthen bowls around the platter contain portions of dal, vegetables, fish, meat, and yogurt.

Wasting food is considered sinful among Indians. Children are taught to eat up everything they have been served, and food is never thrown away. In the villages leftovers are given to animals; in the cities, to servants and street beggars.

A family enjoying a meal in a restaurant.

Eating times vary from region to region. Southern Indians generally do not eat breakfast, but have a very early brunch. Bengalis are known to have dinner very late at night.

TABOOS AND PREFERENCES

Abstinence from food and drink is part and parcel of Indian life. One may fast temporarily or avoid particular foods or both. Most Indians avoid meat on occasion, and many are vegetarian for life. Beef, to Hindus, and pork, to Muslims, are forbidden foods. Muslims eat only halal foods—that is, meat and other edible products made from animals that have been slaughtered in the Islamic way.

Brahmans, some of the Hindu merchant communities, Jains, and many Buddhists are strict lacto-vegetarians. They consume milk products, but avoid eggs, fish, chicken, and meat. Orthodox Brahmans and Jains avoid onions, garlic, coffee, and tea, as all these are believed to activate the baser passions. Strict food habits and a disciplined diet are considered essential for a spiritual life.

INTERNET LINKS

www.indianfoodforever.com

This website introduces the cuisines of India by region, with hundreds of recipes to suit various dietary considerations.

www.food-india.com

This site features recipes as well as articles on a variety of topics such as Indian dining etiquette, ingredients, and street food. It also teaches various cooking techniques of Indian cuisine.

www.india.gov.in/citizen/agriculture/rice.php

This website is devoted to rice cultivation in India, with links to different varieties of rice and how to plant it.

NAAN

This is a baked leavened bread, eaten with a lentil soup, a few meats and vegetables, and some yogurt.

Ingredients

0.25 oz (7 g) active dry yeast

1 cup (250 ml) warm water

¼ cup (62.5 ml) white sugar

3 tablespoons (45 ml) milk

1 egg, beaten

2 teaspoons (10 ml) salt

4½ cups (1.125 kg) bread flour

¼ cup (62.5 ml) butter, melted

2 teaspoons (10 ml) garlic, minced (optional)

Dissolve the yeast in warm water in a large bowl. Let it stand until frothy (about 10 minutes). Stir in the sugar, milk, egg, salt and flour to make a soft dough. Knead the dough until smooth. Do this on a lightly floured surface. Place the dough in a well-oiled bowl and cover it with damp cloth, leaving it aside to rise until it doubles in size (about an hour).

Punch the dough down and knead in the garlic (the garlic is optional). Pull off golf ball sized pieces of dough, roll into balls and leave aside to rise (covered with a damp cloth) until they double in volume (about half an hour). Preheat the grill to high heat.

Using a rolling pin, roll out a ball of dough into a thin disc. Lightly oil the grill. Put the rolled-out dough onto the grill and leave it for about 2—3 minutes or until it begins to puff and turn brown. Brush butter on the uncooked side, and turn the dough over and cook it for about 2—3 minutes.

RASGULLA

This is a very popular cheese-based syrupy sweet dish.

Ingredients

2$\frac{1}{2}$ cups (625 ml) milk

1 cup (250 ml) unflavored yogurt

2 teaspoons (10 ml) lemon juice

$\frac{1}{2}$ teaspoons (2.5 ml) salt

$\frac{3}{4}$ cup (180 ml) chopped almonds

$\frac{2}{3}$ cup (170 ml) semolina flour

3$\frac{3}{4}$ cups (930 ml) water

4 cups (1 kg) sugar

Pinch of cream of tartar

$\frac{1}{2}$ teaspoon (2.5 ml) rose water

Boil milk and add yogurt, lemon juice, and salt. Remove from heat and stir gently until white curds separate from the whey. Strain curdled mixture through a clean piece of cheesecloth until almost dry. Wrap cloth around cheese and place under a heavy weight. Leave to drain for 3 hours. Add almonds and semolina flour and knead into a soft dough. Break dough into 12 to 15 small balls and set aside. Boil water, sugar, and cream of tartar until sugar dissolves. Carefully drop dough balls into syrup and simmer gently for 2 hours. Stir in rose water. Serve hot or cold.

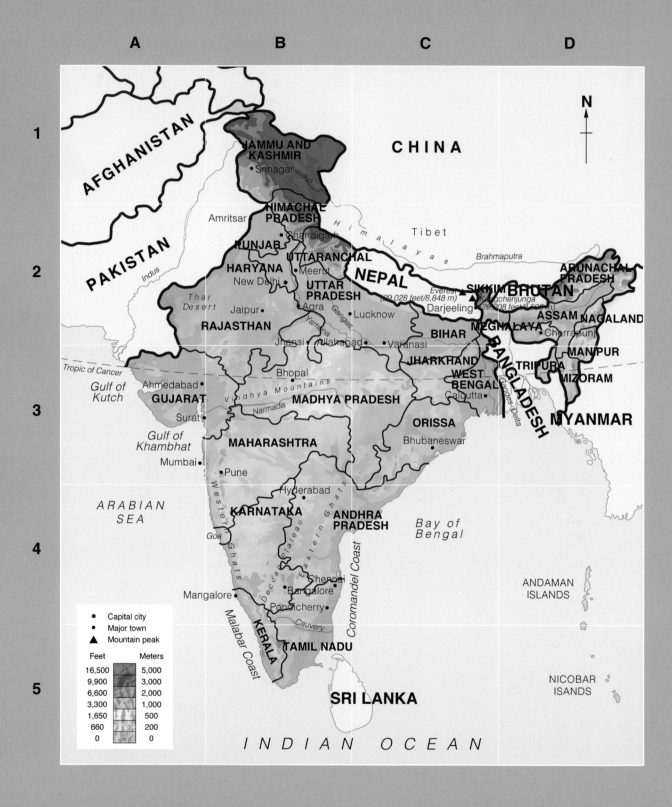

MAP OF INDIA

Afghanistan, A1, A2, B1
Agra, B2
Ahmedabad, A3, B3
Allahabad, C2
Amritsar, B2
Andaman Islands, D4
Andhra Pradesh, B3, B4, C3, C4
Arabian Sea, A2—A4, B4
Arunachal Pradesh, D2
Assam, D2, D3

Bangalore, B4
Bangladesh, C2, C3, D2, D3
Bay of Bengal, C3, C4, D3, D4
Bhopal, B3
Bhutan, C2, D2
Bihar, C2, C3
Brahmaputra River, C2, D2
Bhubaneswar, C3

Calcutta, C3
Cauvery River, B4, B5
Chandigarh, B2
Chennai, B4
Cherrapunji, D2
China, B1, B2, C1, C2, D1, D2
Coromandel Coast, B4, B5

Darjeeling, C2

Deccan Plateau, B4

Eastern Ghats, B4, C3, C4
Everest, C2

Ganges Delta, C3, D3
Ganges River, B2, C2, C3
Goa, B4
Gujarat, A3, B3
Gulf of Khambhat, A3
Gulf of Kutch, A3

Haryana, B2
Himachal Pradesh, B1, B2
Himalayas, B2, C2
Hyderabad, B4

Indian Ocean, A5, B5, C5, D5
Indus River, A1—3, B1, B2, C2

Jaipur, B2
Jammu and Kashmir, B1
Jhansi, B2
Jharkhand, C2, C3

Kangchenjunga, C2
Karnataka, B3, B4
Kerala, B4, B5

Lucknow, C2

Madhya Pradesh, B2, B3, C3

Maharashtra, B3, B4
Malabar Coast, B4, B5
Mangalore, B4
Manipur, D2, D3
Meerut, B2
Meghalaya, D2
Mizoram, D3
Mumbai, A3, B3
Myanmar, D2, D3, D4

Nagaland, D2
Narmada River, B3
Nepal, B2, C2
New Delhi, B2
Nicobar Islands, D5

Orissa, C3, C4

Pakistan, A1, A2, A3, B1, B2
Pondicherry, B4
Pune, B3
Punjab, B2

Rajasthan, A2, A3, B2, B3

Sikkim, C2
Sri Lanka, B5, C5
Srinagar, B1
Surat, B3

Tamil Nadu, B4, B5
Thar Desert, A2, B2
Tibet, B2, C2, D2
Tripura, D3
Tropic of Cancer, A3—D3

Uttaranchal, B2, C2
Uttar Pradesh, B2, B3, C2, C3

Varanasi, C2
Vindhya Mountains, B3

West Bengal, C2, C3, D2, D3
Western Ghats, B3, B4

Yamuna River, B2, C2

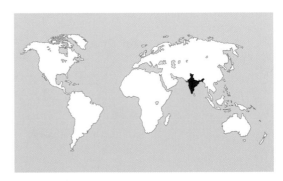

ECONOMIC INDIA

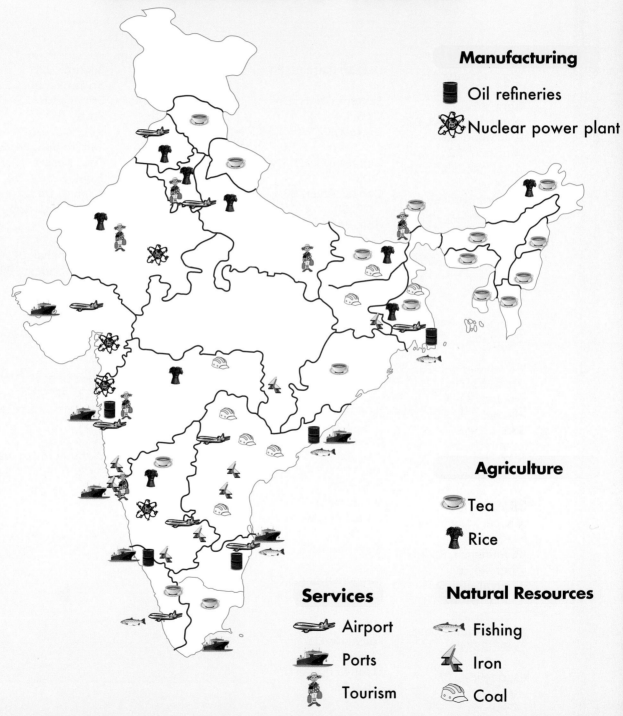

ABOUT THE ECONOMY

OVERVIEW

India is fast becoming an economic powerhouse in Asia. With GDP growth rate exceeding expectations, the country is now one of the top 10 economies in the world. Although most of the working population is employed in agriculture, it is the services sector that brings in the largest revenue, especially the IT industry. This has led to the creation of an affluent middle class, especially in the cities. Poverty, however, is a serious issue, with around 29 percent of the population living below the poverty line, most of them in rural areas. The challenge for the Indian government, in the next decade, is how to bridge the seemingly insurmountable divide between rich and poor and how to enable the poor to share in the newfound wealth of the country.

GROSS DOMESTIC PRODUCT (GDP)

$3.68 trillion (2009 estimate)

GDP PER CAPITA

$3,200 (2009 estimate)

GROWTH RATE

8.6 percent (2010 estimate)

CURRENCY

US$1=44.52 INR (June 2011)
1 INR=100 paise (singular paisa)

INFLATION

10.9 percent (2009 estimate)

MAIN EXPORTS

Agricultural produce, textiles, vehicles, chemicals, leather goods, iron, steel, gems

MAIN IMPORTS

Crude oil and petroleum products, machinery, precious stones, fertilizers, and chemicals

LABOR FORCE

467 million

TOURISM

5.11 million visitors (2009)

MAIN TRADE PARTNERS

China, United States, Saudi Arabia, United Arab Emirates, Australia, Germany, and Singapore

AGRICULTURAL PRODUCTS

Rice, wheat, oilseed, cotton, jute, tea, sugarcane, lentils, onions, potatoes, dairy products, sheep, goats, poultry, fish

NATURAL RESOURCES

Coal (fourth-largest reserves in the world), iron ore, manganese, mica, bauxite, titanium ore, chromite, natural gas, diamonds, petroleum, limestone, and arable land

CULTURAL INDIA

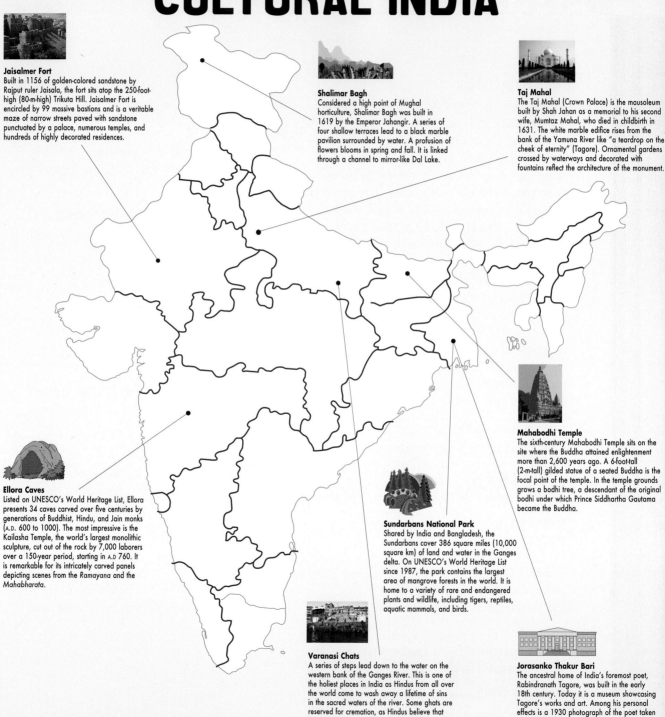

Jaisalmer Fort
Built in 1156 of golden-colored sandstone by Rajput ruler Jaisala, the fort sits atop the 250-foot-high (80-m-high) Trikuta Hill. Jaisalmer Fort is encircled by 99 massive bastions and is a veritable maze of narrow streets paved with sandstone punctuated by a palace, numerous temples, and hundreds of highly decorated residences.

Shalimar Bagh
Considered a high point of Mughal horticulture, Shalimar Bagh was built in 1619 by the Emperor Jahangir. A series of four shallow terraces lead to a black marble pavilion surrounded by water. A profusion of flowers blooms in spring and fall. It is linked through a channel to mirror-like Dal Lake.

Taj Mahal
The Taj Mahal (Crown Palace) is the mausoleum built by Shah Jahan as a memorial to his second wife, Mumtaz Mahal, who died in childbirth in 1631. The white marble edifice rises from the bank of the Yamuna River like "a teardrop on the cheek of eternity" (Tagore). Ornamental gardens crossed by waterways and decorated with fountains reflect the architecture of the monument.

Mahabodhi Temple
The sixth-century Mahabodhi Temple sits on the site where the Buddha attained enlightenment more than 2,600 years ago. A 6-foot-tall (2-m-tall) gilded statue of a seated Buddha is the focal point of the temple. In the temple grounds grows a bodhi tree, a descendant of the original bodhi under which Prince Siddhartha Gautama became the Buddha.

Ellora Caves
Listed on UNESCO's World Heritage List, Ellora presents 34 caves carved over five centuries by generations of Buddhist, Hindu, and Jain monks (A.D. 600 to 1000). The most impressive is the Kailasha Temple, the world's largest monolithic sculpture, cut out of the rock by 7,000 laborers over a 150-year period, starting in A.D 760. It is remarkable for its intricately carved panels depicting scenes from the *Ramayana* and the *Mahabharata*.

Sundarbans National Park
Shared by India and Bangladesh, the Sundarbans cover 386 square miles (10,000 square km) of land and water in the Ganges delta. On UNESCO's World Heritage List since 1987, the park contains the largest area of mangrove forests in the world. It is home to a variety of rare and endangered plants and wildlife, including tigers, reptiles, aquatic mammals, and birds.

Varanasi Chats
A series of steps lead down to the water on the western bank of the Ganges River. This is one of the holiest places in India as Hindus from all over the world come to wash away a lifetime of sins in the sacred waters of the river. Some ghats are reserved for cremation, as Hindus believe that Varanasi is an auspicious place to die.

Jorasanko Thakur Bari
The ancestral home of India's foremost poet, Rabindranath Tagore, was built in the early 18th century. Today it is a museum showcasing Tagore's works and art. Among his personal effects is a 1930 photograph of the poet taken with Albert Einstein.

ABOUT THE CULTURE

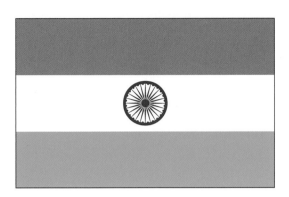

OFFICIAL NAME
Republic of India

CAPITAL
New Delhi

POPULATION
1,173,108,018 (July 2010 estimate)

STATES
Andhra Pradesh, Arunachal Pradesh, Assam, Bihar, Chhatisgarh, Goa, Gujarat, Haryana, Himachal Pradesh, Jammu and Kashmir, Jharkhand, Karnataka, Kerala, Madhya Pradesh, Maharashtra, Manipur, Meghalaya, Mizoram, Nagaland, Orissa, Punjab, Rajasthan, Sikkim, Tamil Nadu, Tripura, Uttarakhand, Uttar Pradesh, West Bengal

UNION TERRITORIES
Andaman & Nicobar Islands, Chandigarh, National Capital Territory (NCT) of New Delhi, Dadra & Nagar Haveli, Daman & Diu, Lakshadweep, Puducherry

MAJOR LANGUAGES
Hindi: 41 percent, Bengali: 8.1 percent, Telugu: 7.2 percent, Marathi: 7 percent, Tamil: 5.9 percent, Urdu: 5 percent, Gujarati: 4.5 percent, Kannada: 3.7 percent, Malayalam: 3.2 percent, Oriya: 3.2 percent, Punjabi: 2.8 percent, Assamese: 1.3 percent, Maithili: 1.2 percent, Others: 5.9 percent

ETHNIC GROUPS
Indo-Aryan 72 percent, Dravidian 25 percent, Mongoloid and others 3 percent (2000)

MAJOR RELIGIONS
Hindu: 80.5 percent, Muslim: 13.4 percent, Christian: 2.3 percent, Sikh: 1.9 percent, Others: 1.8 percent, unspecified: 0.1 percent (2001 census)

BIRTHRATE
21.34 births/1,000 population (2010 estimate)

DEATH RATE
7.53 deaths/1,000 population (July 2010 estimate)

INFANT MORTALITY RATE
Total: 49.13 deaths/1,000 live births
Male: 47.7 deaths/1,000 live births
Female: 50.73 deaths/1,000 live births (2010 estimate)

LIFE EXPECTANCY
Total population: 66.46 years; Male: 65.46 years; Female: 67.57 years (2010 estimate)

TIME LINE

IN INDIA	IN THE WORLD
	1206–1368
1510	Genghis Khan unifies the Mongols and starts conquest of the world. At its height, the Mongol Empire under Kublai Khan stretches from China to Persia and parts of Europe and Russia.
Portuguese forces capture Goa.	
1686	
English war with the Mughals	
1757	**1776**
Battle of Plassey in Bengal; British rule in India begins.	U.S. Declaration of Independence
1858	**1789–99**
East India Company dissolves; Mughal Empire ends.	The French Revolution
1885	
The Indian National Congress forms.	
1905	
Bengal partitions into East and West.	**1914**
	World War I begins.
	1939
	World War II begins.
	1945
1947	The United States drops atomic bombs on Hiroshima and Nagasaki. World War II ends.
India gains independence; Jawaharlal Nehru becomes first prime minister; war with Pakistan starts in October and ends in December 1948.	
1948	
Mahatma Gandhi is assassinated.	
1965	
Second war with Pakistan	
1971	
Third war with Pakistan	
1984	
Prime Minister Indira Gandhi is assassinated.	
1991	
Former prime minister Rajiv Gandhi is assassinated; P. V. Narasimha Rao is elected India's ninth prime minister.	

IN INDIA	IN THE WORLD
1996 • Atal Bihari Vajpayee becomes prime minister; he resigns after 13 days in office.	
1997 •• Kicheril Raman Narayanan is made president.	**1997** Hong Kong is returned to China.
1998 • Vajpayee returns as prime minister; India declares itself a nuclear power.	
2001 •• Massive earthquake rocks Gujarat, killing more than 20,000 people and injuring 167,000 others.	**2001** Terrorists crash planes into New York, Washington D.C., and Pennsylvania.
	2003 War in Iraq begins.
2004 •• Asian tsunami batters eastern and southern coasts of India and Andaman & Nicobar Islands.	**2004** Eleven Asia countries are hit by giant tsunami, killing at least 225,000 people.
	2005 Hurricane Katrina devastates the Gulf Coast of the United States.
2006 • Terrorist attacks on Mumbai trains leave more than 200 dead.	
2007 • Islamist militants bomb train traveling from Delhi to Lahore; India's first woman president, Pratibha Devisingh Patil, is sworn in.	
2008 •• India launches its first unmanned mission to the moon; series of coordinated attacks on Mumbai landmarks last three days, killing more than 173 people.	**2008** Earthquake in Sichuan, China, kills 67,000 people.
2009 •• Congress-led alliance gains overwhelming support in national elections.	**2009** Outbreak of flu virus H1N1 around the world
	2011 Twin earthquake and tsunami disasters strike northeast Japan, leaving over 14,000 dead and thousands more missing.

GLOSSARY

Aryan
Indian race of mixed origin; Indo-European

burka
Head-to-toe veil worn by traditional Muslim women

caste
Social class, originally based on occupation. Examples are the Brahmans (priests), Kshatriya (ruling class), Vaishyas (merchants), and Sudras (laborers)

Dravidian
Indigenous Indian ethnicity

gotra (go-trah)
One's ancestral lineage

Hanafi
One of four teachings of the Sunni sect

Harijan (hah-ri-jahn)
Children of god. The name given by Mahatma Gandhi to the "outcastes" known as the untouchables

Hindu Trinity
Brahma the creator, Vishnu the preserver, and Shiva the destroyer

jati (jah-ti)
A clan

kangri (KAHNG-gree)
An earthen pot of hot coal used by Kashmiris to keep warm in winter

karma
A fundamental Hindu and Buddhist belief similar to the principle of cause and effect

maharaja
An Indian prince

maulvi (mole-vee)
Muslim priest

moksha (mohk-shah)
Hindu equivalent of the Buddhist nirvana—the release of the soul from the life cycle

panchayats (PEHN-chah-yehts)
Village and district courts

satyagraha (SEHT-yah-grah-hah)
The nonviolent fight for justice advocated by Mahatma Gandhi

Sunni law
Islamic law based on the word of the Prophet Muhammad, but not attributed to him

Taj Mahal
The magnificent marble mausoleum in the city of Agra known as the eighth wonder of the world

Vedas
Books of Knowledge. Sacred writings composed around 1500 B.C. Mainly Rig Veda, Sama Veda, Atharva Veda, Yajur Veda, Brahmanas, and Upanishads. *Veda* means "knowledge" in Sanskrit

FOR FURTHER INFORMATION

BOOKS

India. London: DK Publishing, 2008.

Jaffrey, Madhur. *Climbing the Mango Trees: A Memoir of a Childhood in India*. London: Vintage Books, 2007.

Milbourne, Anna. *Stories from India*. London: Usborne Books, 2006.

Roy, Arundhati. *The God of Small Things*. New York: Random House, 2008.

Seabrook, Jeremy and Imran Ahmed Siddiqui. *People without History: India's Muslim Ghettos*. London: Pluto Press, 2011.

Seale, Shelley. *The Weight of Silence: Invisible Children of India*. Hot Springs, South Dakota: Dog's Eye View Media, 2009.

MUSIC

Kosmic Artists. *Sacred Chants of Ancient India*. Kosmic Music, 2007.

Lata Mangeshkar. *Legend: India's Best-Loved Singer*. Manteca, 2006.

Ravi Shankar. *Sounds of India*. Sbme Special Mkts, 2008.

Various artists. *Mystic India*. New Earth, 2001.

Various artists. *Devotion: Religious Chants from India*. Arc Music, 2006.

FILMS

Ancient India: A Journey Back in Time (Lost Treasures of the Ancient World). Cromwell Productions. 2006.

Ashutosh Gowariker. *Lagaan—Once Upon a Time in India*. Sony Pictures, 2002.

Tom Hugh-Jones. *Ganges*. BBC Warner, 2008.

BIBLIOGRAPHY

BOOKS

Cummings, David. *India*. New York: Bookwright Press, 1989.

Stewart, Gail. *India*. New York: Maxwell Macmillan International, 1992.

WEBSITES

Central Intelligence Agency World Factbook: India. www.cia.gov/cia/publications/factbook/geos/in.html

Government of India. www.indiagov.org

Incredible India. www.incredibleindia.org

Internet Indian History Sourcebook. www.fordham.edu/halsall/india/indiasbook.html

Lonely Planet World Guide: Destination India. www.lonelyplanet.com/destinations/indian_subcontinent/india/guides.htm

MapsofIndia.com. www.mapsofindia.com

INDEX

INDEX